The Authorities

Powerful Wisdom from Leaders in the Field

JACEK SIWEK

Award Winning Author

AuthoritiesPress

Publisher
Authorities Press
Markham, ON
Canada

Printed in the United States and Canada.

FOREWORD

Experts are to be admired for their knowledge, but they often remain unrecognized by the general public because they save their information and insights for paying customers and clients. There are many experts in a given field, but their impact is limited to the handful of people with whom they work.

Unlike experts, authorities share their knowledge and expertise far more broadly, so they make a big impact on the world. Authorities become known and admired as leading experts and, as such, typically do very well economically and professionally. Most authorities are also mature enough to know that part of the joy of monetary success is the accompanying moral and spiritual obligation to give back.

Many people want to learn and work with well-respected and generous authorities, but don't always know where to find them. They may be known to their peers, or within a specific community, but have not had the opportunity to reach a wider audience. At one time, they might have submitted a proposal to the For Dummies or Chicken Soup for the Soul series of books, but it's now almost impossible to get accepted as a new author in such branded book series.

It is more than fitting that Raymond Aaron, an internationally known and respected authority in his own right, would be the one to recognize the need for a new venue in which authorities could share their considerable knowledge with readers everywhere. As the only author ever to be included in both of the book series mentioned above, Raymond has had the opportunity to give back and he understands how crucial it is for authorities to have a platform from which to share their expertise.

I

I have known and worked with Raymond for a number of years and consider him a valued friend and talented coach. He knows how to spot talented and knowledgeable people and he desires to see them prosper. Over the years, success coaching and speaking engagements around the world have made it possible for Raymond to meet many of these talented authorities. He recognizes and relates to their passion and enthusiasm for what they do, as well as their desire to share what they know. He tells me that's why he created this new nonfiction branded book series, The Authorities.

Dr. Nido Qubein
President, High Point University

TABLE OF CONTENTS

INTRODUCTION

This book introduces you to *The Authorities* — individuals who have distinguished themselves in life and in business. Authorities make a big impact on the world. Authorities are leaders in their chosen fields. Authorities typically do very well financially, and are evolved enough to know that part of the joy of monetary success is the accompanying social, moral and spiritual obligation to give back.

Authorities are not just outstanding. They are also *known* to be outstanding.

This additional element begins to explain the difference between two strategic business and life concepts — one that seems great, but isn't, and the other that fills in the essential missing gap of the first.

The first concept is "the expert."

What is an expert? The real definition is …

EXPERT: *a person who knows stuff*

People who have attained a very senior academic degree (like a PhD or an MD) definitely know stuff. People who read voraciously and retain what they read definitely know stuff. Unfortunately, just because you know stuff does not mean that anyone respects the fact that you do. Even though some experts are successful, alas, most are not — because knowing stuff is not enough.

Well, then, what is the missing piece?

What the expert lacks, "the authority" has. The authority both knows stuff and is *known* to know stuff. So, more simply …

AUTHORITY: *a person who is known as an expert*

The difference is not subtle. The difference is not merely semantic. The difference is enormous.

When it comes to this subject, there are actually three categories in which people fall:

- People who don't know much and are unsuccessful in life and in business. Most people fall in this category.

- People who know stuff, but still don't leave much of a footprint in the world. There are a lot of people like this.

- Experts who are also *known* as experts become authorities and authorities are always wondrously successful. Authorities are able to contribute more to humanity through both their chosen work and their giving back.

This book is about the highest category, *The Authorities* — people who have reached the peak in their field and are known as such.

Some authorities in this book you will know. You have learned from them in the past, and you are looking forward to what they share in this book. Others like Jacek Siwek, you may not have had the opportunity to gain knowledge from.

Jacek Siwek, a Polish immigrant to Canada, has written a powerful metaphor called *Immigrating to Success*. It's an idea that making life-changing decisions won't be easy but will be worth every effort.

When someone immigrates, commitment is a must. You can't just turn around and go home. No, you leave friends and family and familiar places behind. Most often you have very little money, and you may not even know the language. The obstacles that lay before you are seemingly impossible, but you have no choice but to succeed; your bridges have been burned.

Immigration, in fact, is a point of no return. An immigrant makes it happen no matter how hard it gets or how long it takes. It's only when you decide with the same amount of certainty to immigrate to success that you have a chance to transform your life.

Jacek begins his metaphor by having you choose a destination—a goal you want to achieve, no matter the cost. Next he has you educate yourself with the four stages of learning. Unexpectedly, he then talks about the importance of humility during your journey. He makes a moving argument for it. Using another metaphor, Jacek also writes about removing the "dirt" from your life as a way of clearing a pathway to success. Communication and rapport-building skills are also a must for any immigrant. This is no different for the pursuer of success.

Success always comes with a high price tag. That's just the way it is. Jacek points out that we must understand and learn to let go of the pain that is part and parcel of the price of admission.

One of the most valuable gifts Jacek Siwek gives you is a comparison between the habitual behaviours of successful people and unsuccessful people. This comprehensive lists shows you there are two different cultures with different beliefs, values, rituals, and habits. The items in the "successful list" are the fundamentals that must be learned and practiced in the support network you must build.

There are several other important revelations in *Immigrating to Success*, and I encourage you to read it and put these things into practice.

They are *The Authorities*. Learn from them. Connect with them. Let them uplift you. Learning from them and working with them is the secret ingredient for success which may well allow you to rise to the level of Authority soon.

To be considered for inclusion in a subsequent edition of *The Authorities*, register to attend a future event at www.aaron.com/events where you will be interviewed and considered.

Immigrating to Success

Self-Leadership Strategies to Manifest Your Life Long Dreams

JACEK SIWEK

Immigration requires more than interest, it requires commitment. If you want to immigrate to success, commitment is a must.

Some decisions in life make little difference, others will turn your life around entirely. For example, a decision to immigrate is definitely a life-changing decision. I left Poland and immigrated to Canada in 1996. My whole life changed in just one day. I had to learn a new language and culture, gain new friends, learn how to live in a big city, and the list goes on and on. However, there was one more decision I made that had a significant impact on my life. It was the decision to be successful. It wasn't an easy journey, but now that I look back in time, I see how immigrating to another country and changing my life from poverty to success resemble each other remarkably. Allow me to explain.

Immigration is a point of no return. It's not a short visit to see how things will work out. If it gets hard you can't go back. An immigrant makes it happen no matter how hard it gets or how long it takes. It's only when you decide with the same amount of certainty to immigrate to success do you have a chance to transform your life.

Why do people immigrate? Most do it to stop or avoid pain. There's a moment in life when you realize that the past was horrible, the present is even more painful, and the future looks worse. At that moment you decide to change. At that moment there's a psychological shift when you say "No more! Not another day of this! This must change and I must change it!"

If I can teach you any lesson about pain, it would be this: pain is the greatest teacher and motivator of all. If you want to succeed in life, you must first get dissatisfied with your current situation. You must experience massive, immediate, enormous, unbearable amounts of pain in order to be able to come to the moment when you realize "This must change!"

If you aren't where you want to be with your finances CHANGE IT. If you aren't where you want to be with your body weight CHANGE IT. If you aren't happy with your job CHANGE IT. If you aren't happy with your relationship CHANGE IT.

Don't get me wrong, I'm all for making the best out of what we have, but far too often I've seen people who suffer being together. I know it's not easy, but it all comes down to that moment of asking "How long do I want to tolerate it?" In life we get what we tolerate, so if you see something isn't working and you keep tolerating it, nothing will change. You must reach the point of no return, the moment when you decide that not another day will pass by with you living like this. This is the perfect moment when you must immigrate to success. There's no better way.

DEFINE YOUR DESTINATION

In order to reach your goal of immigrating to success you must:

1. Clearly define your goals. Define what you want, not what you don't want. You must know exactly when your goal has been achieved.

2. State what you are committed to do in order to achieve your goals.

3. Name the price you are willing to pay to get there (in terms of time, money, and sacrifice).

4. Get rid of old habits that stop you.

5. Identify what it will cost you not to get to where you want to go. What would be the ultimate pain of not getting there?

6. Define who you want to become as a result of achieving this goal.

If you have all those points done your next step is to educate yourself.

FOUR STAGES OF LEARNING

1. *First, you don't know what you don't know.* For example, you have never seen or heard of a car. How could you learn to drive one? You have no clue what it is. Similarly, you might be ignorant to things that could be useful. Someone else must show you what you don't know. Keep your mind open to other possibilities. Remember, you don't have all the

answers.

2. *Second, you know what you didn't know.* At this stage you're discovering the things you weren't aware of. You don't have any skills yet, but you know what you have to learn in order to succeed. For example, you know what a car is and you've seen people driving one, though you have never driven one yourself. In order for you to learn new skills you must not be afraid to ask for help.

3. *Third, you know what you didn't know and you're actually physically doing it.* At this stage you are actively doing what you know, but it takes your full attention. At this stage it will require your entire focus to complete the task. For example, you know what a car is and you know how to drive it, but it takes your full attention and you aren't capable of doing anything else while driving. Now your focus is on your goal, but it's still outside yourself.

4. *Fourth, you are no longer thinking about what you're doing, you're doing it automatically.* At this stage, because of repetition, your subconscious mind is no longer requiring your full attention and focus. You can do the task while focusing on something else. For example, you can drive, but your focus is on something else. You can have a conversation with somebody sitting next to you. You can listen to the radio or you can plan your next day. Your subconscious mind takes over the complex process of operating a vehicle and simplifies it into one task called driving. We call it second nature because we can perform it without our full attention.

HUMILITY

"Be all that you can be." "You're the best." "You can do anything you put your mind to." "Believe in yourself." "You are worth it." We keep hearing these phrases over and over again. You'll find them on the internet, Facebook, YouTube videos, and inside self-improvement books. But what about humility? What is humility? Humility is not thinking less of yourself, but rather it's thinking of yourself less. Read the above sentence a few times until it sinks in. Humility is the greatest friend in your progress and learning.

In the process of immigrating there's something I refer to as you don't know what you already know. It sounds strange, but I'll give you an example. You are quite capable of asking for directions in your own language. However, when you don't know the foreign language it becomes a challenge. Successful people use different language for the same things. They just sometimes use a sophisticated vocabulary. This kind of thing is common in the financial, medical, and legal industries. So when you start spending time with successful people and they use vocabulary you don't understand, do not be discouraged. Chances are you know exactly what they are talking about, but you simply don't know the verbal representations of the discussed topics. Do not be afraid of asking for clarifications.

I know it is humiliating when learning a new language to ask the same question over and over again. You feel stupid asking for something you think you should know by now. But that fear of appearing stupid, that fear of what people will think if you ask this question again, will prevent you from progressing forward. Recognizing this helped me to learn the language and culture faster than many of my peers at the same time. You must know that you need to put your focus on the other person and ask repeatedly for help until you learn those things necessary to succeed. We have to embarrass ourselves many times and be okay with it. We have to give ourselves time to make mistakes—lots and lots of mistakes. If we do, we will progress 100 times faster than those proud people who are too afraid to sound dumb. That's humility working for you.

Being afraid of making mistakes, and looking stupid because of it, is one of the top reasons people don't succeed. If you study successful people you will see a common pattern. They all make a lot of mistakes, experience plenty of failures, feel a lot of embarrassment, and experience a lot of setbacks. If we want to succeed, we must be ready to accept failure as a major part of our path. However, every time you feel like quitting know that there's another person who already quit right behind you. If you keep going forward, there will be fewer people and less competition simply because the reasons they stopped did not stop you. One of the major reasons why people give up or don't try in the first place is because of fear of being humiliated. They don't want people to criticize them, and they don't want people to make fun of them. Nobody does. But the truth is this is your life, and there will always be people who will make fun of you. There will always be people who'll think badly of you, criticize you, and point the finger at you. It's absolutely inevitable. Remember, humility is all about thinking of yourself less, rather than thinking less of yourself.

DIRT REMOVAL

"Bad habits are easier to abandon today than tomorrow."
– Proverb

This step is a must, but you may not appreciate its value until you start putting it in practice. Every house that ever got built started with someone's vision, then a blueprint was made. As much as most want to see the completed version of their beautiful kitchen or bathroom, the first step of construction is removal of dirt. In order to build solid foundations, you must remove all loose soil. You want to build up but first you must go down to the solid place that will not move when storms and winters come. Removal of dirt in your life is no different. We all have it and we must get rid of as much of it as we can in order to build ourselves based on solid value.

Here are some things that might be in your life that aren't allowing you to build the life you want to have:

1. Negative people and their negative comments and criticisms

2. Media. Example: Constant Negative News (CNN)

3. Time wasters: games, social media, TV, excessive entertainment

4. Unfinished projects (like a book you started reading and haven't finished)

5. Disorganized messes (like keys you've never used and don't even know what they're for)

6. Junk food

Removing dirt from your life comes down to one word: STANDARD. You have a standard in life that you'll not go below. A standard is nothing more than a line in the sand that says "I'm not willing to go below this. It's unacceptable, and I refuse to tolerate it." In life we will get what we tolerate, so setting up a minimum standard is a necessity. When I immigrated, all I had with me was one suitcase with summer clothes. When you immigrate, you have to be careful about what you take with you because your allowance for your luggage is limited. At the same time, you'll realize just how few things you really need and that leaving stuff behind might be one of the best things that could happen to free you from having to deal with unnecessary time wasters.

In your new country of success there's simply no space for time wasting activities and negative people.

COMMUNICATE TO INFLUENCE

Every person who ever immigrated to another country knows how difficult it is until they learn the language people use to communicate. If you can't speak the language, your communication will be extremely limited, and as a result your life will always be a struggle. In fact, should someone ask me what the number one skill in life is, I will say without hesitation: "You must master communication skills in order to be successful."

Think about it for a moment. Show me one aspect of your life where proper communication isn't required in order to be successful. If you want to be a successful parent, you must first learn how to communicate with your children. If you want to be a successful spouse, you must learn how to communicate with your partner. If you want to be successful in business, you must learn how to effectively communicate with your customers, employees, business partners, investors, and the list goes on.

However, the most important person you must master communication with is yourself. You have to learn how to communicate with yourself in order to stay motivated, focused, driven, dedicated, and committed. You must know what works for you and what doesn't. You must become a student of yourself first before you learn what motivates others. Language is what connects people, but lack of it separates them. You should put in the effort necessary to learn what you need to know in order to become an effective communicator. Who is an effective communicator? It's a person who can influence others to take action. In order to influence you need to learn how to connect with others first, which means you have to learn how to develop rapport.

MAGIC OF RAPPORT

The key to rapport lies in one word: commonality. I can summarize this skill with one sentence: people like each other when they're like each other. The more you have in common with others the easier it is to develop rapport. Maybe you had a situation when you met someone for the first time and you kept asking questions to find something in common. If you found nothing, then the conversation became awkward and most likely died. Maybe you've known someone for many years and still can't find anything in common, so each time you see each other you feel like you are total strangers. However, I'm also sure you've had a moment in life when you met someone for the first time and instantly felt a connection. After a short period of time you felt like you had known that person forever. Why does that happen? Well, you simply saw yourself in the other person. You liked them because they were like you or they were similar to someone you already liked.

This is all based on commonality. Your subconscious mind will quickly pick up on all the similarities between the person you just met and yourself. If you know nothing of the person you just met, all you have to do is match and mirror them as closely as you can. Immediately match their physiology by copying their body language. If they sit on a chair, you sit on a chair. If they lean forward, you lean forward. If they have crossed legs, you cross yours. Simply match and mirror what they do and their mind will soon start picking up a signal that you are just like them. As soon as they start speaking, match their speaking pattern. If they speak slow, you speak slow. If they speak fast, you speak with the same tempo. You might be afraid they'll notice what you are doing and will accuse you of mimicking them. Truthfully, they won't notice. Especially because they don't know you yet and they don't know your natural behavior. Therefore, the more you copy them the quicker rapport will be developed.

9

If you use this method daily, sooner or later it will become second nature and you'll be able to develop rapport with people instantaneously without ever worrying about what you'll have to say or how to behave.

PAIN OF LETTING GO

"Sometimes we have to let go of what is good in order to be great."
– Unknown

This moment hits every immigrant on the planet: feeling homesick. It can be missing loved ones, friends, familiar places, or favorite TV shows in your own language. I was not immune to it. I fell in love with a girl right before I immigrated and I missed her a lot. I missed my best friend and our daily walks to school. I missed my town and the street I grew up on. Most of all I missed the feeling of belonging. Everyone has to go through it, but it doesn't make it easier just because others feel the same pain. There were many moments when I felt like just jumping on a plane and going back. Feeling like you want to quit because you feel like you don't belong is normal and eventually will fade away. When you realize that you no longer want to live a life of poverty you'll have to let go of many things, including the ones you love. During the really tough moments when I worked 14 hour days delivering flyers for $2.50 per hour (minimum wage was $8) I kept in mind one thought that kept me going. In order to be great you have to let go of what is good. There's a price to pay for everything and when you immigrate to a new country or to success you will pay a price. There'll be people in your life who were your close friends, and now that you're having success, they won't want to be around you or you won't want to be around them. There'll be people who'll not be happy about your success, not because they don't care about you but because they don't want to be left behind. You'll discover that people who claimed to be your close friends are now starting to see you as an opportunity for their own gain. There'll be moments when you might want to sabotage your success because you'll feel that it's not worth the trouble you're having. But, if you give up struggling for your success, you'll never get there and as a result, you'll never help anyone else to get there either.

Success comes with a price tag and in order to get it there's no other way than to pay the price. However, there's a moment when you'll know how great of a decision you've made by leaving your old way of living and deciding to immigrate. It's the moment when you go back for a visit. After five years of being in Canada, I finally got my papers, so I decided to go back to Poland for a visit. I was sure that all my peers would be far ahead of me because the previous five years I had spent learning how to live again from scratch. Surely a new language, culture, school, group of friends, etc. would have caused me to grow slower than my peers who kept on going. Or so I thought. When I went back, I quickly realized how much I had grown. I saw how many people were still stuck in the same place and had done nothing with their life. If anything, many were worse off than they had been five years previously. This short visit gave me a lot to think about. All of a sudden all the things I missed had smaller value. I still missed my friends and family, but I knew that if I stayed with them my life would never grow forward at the speed it was growing.

One day we went climbing mountains in Poland and came up with an idea to go see Mount Everest the following weekend. Surely enough, the next weekend we were in Nepal looking at the tallest mountain, riding elephants in a jungle, and trekking in one of the most beautiful regions in the world. My peers couldn't even dream about such an adventure. It was then that I realized it all comes down to answering one question: Is it worth it? If the answer is yes, then simply make a decision, find out what it takes, and go for it.

You've most likely heard of people saying that true friends are found in need. Pain or trouble in life will show who your true friends are. There is truth to that, however, success will show you the same. If someone is your true friend, they'll be happy for you when they see you succeeding. Those are the friends you should keep and cherish. Focus on what you've gained and what the true rewards are for your hard work. Your pain of regret will disappear.

ADAPTING TO A NEW CULTURE

"Well, the thing that I learned as a diplomat is that
human relations ultimately make a huge difference."
– Madeleine Albright, the first female U.S. Secretary of State

When you listen to many motivational speakers, some of the most common advice they'll give you is: You have to stand out. You have to be different. You can't be average. Break some rules, etc. There is definitely truth to that, but what they rarely tell you is that in order for you to become valuable you must first learn, practice, and master the fundamentals. What that means is when you immigrate to a new culture you have to learn how they live and do things before you introduce anything new. Simply put, you have to fit in before you stand out.

Gold fish will grow proportionally to the size of the container you put them in. The bigger the container the bigger the fish will grow. We, too, adapt. We want to fit in and be accepted by those we love. Fitting in is by far one of the most powerful internal motivators we have. I'm sure you've heard that we become the average of five of our closest friends. This is a very true statement. Adapting to a new culture first requires choosing the right culture for you. Your friends will create pressure inside you. This internal pressure will become a driving force for you and it could serve you or destroy you.

When a young person goes through army training, they'll often adopt standards and discipline like nowhere else. Very often they'll even keep making their bed and polishing their shoes when they go home where there's no one to ask them to do these things. However, the more time passes the more such useful habits fade away. Why does this happen? Many studies show that people become what their peer group expects them to. That's why choosing the right peer group is so important. This piece of information is so crucial that if you forgot everything else in this chapter and only learned and applied this one principle, your chances of success would be much greater than if you applied everything else in this chapter except this rule.

Nobody successful builds anything meaningful by themselves. You must learn how to build a team of people who have the same vision and surround yourself with those who'll support you on your goals. There's simply no other way. The question is: How do you find people who live in a "successful country?"

Here are some of the things that successful people do versus those who are not:

SUCCESSFUL PEOPLE	UNSUCCESSFUL PEOPLE
Read every day	Watch TV every day
Compliment	Criticize
Embrace change	Fear change
Forgive others	Hold a grudge

SUCCESSFUL PEOPLE	UNSUCCESSFUL PEOPLE
Talk about ideas	Talk about people
Continuously learn	Think they know it all
Accept responsibility for their failures	Blame others for their failures
Have a sense of gratitude	Have a sense of entitlement
Set goals and develop a written life plan	Never set goals
Journal	Claim they journal but never do
Set a budget	Never set a budget
Save money	Spend money rashly
Have mentors and coaches	Have friends to entertain themselves
Hope others will succeed	Hope others will fail
Operate from a transformational perspective	Operate from a transactional perspective
Give other people credit for their victories	Take all the credit for their victories
Share information and data	Hold information and data
Know who they are and who they are not	Not sure who they are
Know their purpose	Don't know their purpose
Exude joy	Exude anger
Wake up early, go to bed early	Wake up late, go to bed late
Listen to educational programs	Listen to news
In control of their life	Out of control of their life
Manage energy	Manage time
Make to be lists	Make to do lists
Certain, focused, outcome oriented	Uncertain, confused, excuses oriented
On track	Lost

SUCCESSFUL PEOPLE	UNSUCCESSFUL PEOPLE
Know realistically where they are in life and where they want to be at a specific point in time	They think they are much further in life than reality and don't know where they want to be
Take care of their body	Pay attention to their body when they get sick
Anticipate change	React to change
They lead by example	They demand from others
They appreciate others, expect from themselves	They expect of others, appreciate nobody
Build themselves by building others	Try to build themselves by putting others down
Train, practice, memorize	Hope to improvise
They say: Thank you for...(doing or being something specific)	They say: Thank you for everything
Know what they want and focus on it	Know what they don't want and focus on it
Speak the truth with consequence	Justify, talk about excuses, lie to get away
Pay full attention	Distracted
They see challenges in life that make them stronger	They see problems in life that make them weaker
Over deliver and exceed people's expectations	Overpromise and under deliver
They keep changing to get better results	They stay the same expecting better results
If something must change I have to change it	If something must change someone else must change it for me
They celebrate their successes	They celebrate holidays only
They have a story of becoming a victor	They have a story of becoming a victim

As you can see these are two different cultures with different beliefs, values, rituals, and habits. The items in the "successful list" are the fundamentals that must be learned and practiced in your network. You might not be able to check off all the things on the list, but the more you do and the more you put them into practice, the quicker you will get where you want to go.

SHORTCUTS THAT SLOW THINGS DOWN

"Strength and growth come only through continuous effort and struggle."
– Napoleon Hill

What do you think will help you learn a new language: a dictionary or an electronic translator? Many choose the electronic translator because of speed and convenience. Unfortunately, it slows down their progress and impedes their ability to memorize necessary words. Personally, I noticed I had to check a new word two to three times in a dictionary in order to remember it. The electronic translator did the thinking for me so I had to translate the same word many times and even after translating it eight or ten times it still wouldn't stick in my memory. Today, we can use GPS, Google, smart phones, etc., and they're truly great tools. However, they don't train us. By using them our skills aren't getting stronger, they're getting weaker. It's like going to the gym and asking someone to lift the weights for you in the hope that you will develop muscles.

In business, to become an expert, you must start by becoming an apprentice. There's no shortcut. Although, if you just read the headlines on social media, I'm sure you'll find countless examples of people promising you how to become rich instantly by following some simple, secret formula. The truth is, success requires hard work. You must also determine what kind of work is worth your effort. Far too many people fall into the trap of thinking that hard work will bring them success. All you have to do is go to a third world country and watch people working on farms to know this isn't true. They aren't rich but they work very hard.

In business, you will find story after story of people trying to scam others by overcharging and not delivering the value they promised. I have never met a person who successfully scammed others long-term. It's all about producing value in other people's lives. It's about delivering more than what people expect. It's about making someone's life better by creating value for those who need it. There's no shortcut. That's why so many businesses go bankrupt in a very short time. They don't want to take the time to build a brand with a solid foundation that represents value. When the storm hits, they get wiped out.

The struggle is real and in order to succeed you have to invest in yourself. It's by far the most important investment you will ever make. Create a map of what it takes to be successful. Go to school, take courses, read books, go to seminars, take on an apprenticeship, and acquire certifications. I don't know what it will take for you to become successful, but whatever it is you must make a point of identifying where you are, where you want to be, and the best path to get there. You don't have to learn everything, but you do need to know the things you can't outsource to others.

Creating a team is very important and hiring people will definitely be part of your success, but don't expect to just hire people to do things for you and hope they will create success for you. If you want success you have to become a leader, and leaders walk first.

There is one investment that will save you time, money, and lots of frustrations. It's the only "shortcut" that I know of that actually works. It's called modelling.

MODELLING SUCCESS IS THE NEW TIME MACHINE

"Remembering that I'll be dead soon is the most important tool I've ever encountered to help me make the big choices in life. Because almost everything—all external expectations, all pride, all fear of embarrassment or failure—these things just fall away in the face of death, leaving only what is truly important."
– Steve Jobs

Wisdom comes from experience. Experience comes from making mistakes and learning from them. The more mistakes you make, the wiser you will become. But, it's always better to learn from other people's mistakes. Coaching or mentoring can save you decades of mistakes. If you don't have money or connections to successful people, then books and biographies of those who inspire you is a great place to start.

There's access to almost anything we want at our fingertips and we can use NET (No Extra Time) to acquire this knowledge. Listen to audio books in the car, for example. Just add to your existing routine. Don't waste time by learning through trial and error, that's how our parents learned. We simply don't have that much time to waste. Time is our greatest commodity and it should never be wasted. You think you have time but the greatest lesson from death is that you don't. There's no reset button. There's no way of going back and there's no reason to waste your life on unnecessary activities. How much is your time worth? If you're wasting lots of time on a job you hate and at home you only watch TV to escape reality, then you are committing a slow suicide. That's right, your time is limited.

IF YOU KILL YOUR TIME, YOU'RE KILLING YOUR LIFE!

Don't try to be smarter than experts. Follow everything they do until you become an expert yourself, then you can start breaking some rules. Imagine, someone spent 20 years writing a book by gathering the best possible information from their life experience and then you read it in just a few days or sometimes hours. You can compress decades into days by learning from the masters. Can you imagine someone learning computer programming without any guidance? By the time they master the program, their skills will no longer be useful because a new program will take its place. We live in times when we no longer have the luxury of learning slowly. Businesses go bankrupt and get downsized and outsourced every day. Mostly, it's because they failed to innovate and hire consultants that could get them to the new goal faster. Someone else did and beat them to it. Today, making the best use of your time is what makes the difference between winning or losing, between succeeding and failing, between thriving and getting by.

The point of all this talk about time is simple: If you cherish your life and want to be successful, you must have a mentor or a coach. A mentor will give you a totally new perspective on things and could save you years of your life and lots of money in the process. No matter how smart you think you are, you're limited by your opinion and your own perspective. If you watch professional athletes, they all, without exception, have coaches. All famous actors, musicians, politicians, business owners, etc. have coaches and mentors. Many of them have multiple coaches at the same time simply because they know the value of it. Why reinvent the wheel if you can learn from someone who already made all the mistakes and walked the path you want to walk?

If you're serious about success, then you must immigrate to it. If you value your life, get a mentor.

Should you wish to learn more, contact Jacek Siwek at **immigratetosuccess@gmail.com** or visit his website at **www.immigratetosuccess.com**

Step Into Greatness

LES BROWN

You have greatness within you. You can do more than you could ever imagine. The problem most people have is that they set a goal and then ask "how can I do it? I don't have the necessary skills or education or experience".

I know what that's like. I wasted 14 years on asking myself how I could be a motivational speaker. My mind focused on the negative—on the things that were in my way, rather than on the things that were not.

It's not what you don't have but what you think you need that keeps you from getting what you want from life. But, when the dream is big enough, the obstacles don't matter. You'll get there if you stay the course. Nothing can stop you but death itself.

Think about that last statement for a minute. There's nothing on this earth that can stop you from achieving what it is that you want. So, get out of your way, and quit sabotaging your dreams. Do everything in your power to make them happen—because you cannot fail!

They say the best way to die is with your loved ones gathered around your bed. But what if you were dying and it was the ideas you never acted upon, the gifts you never used and the dreams you never pursued, that were circled around your bed? Answer that question right now. Write down your answers. If you die this very moment what ideas, what gifts, what dreams will die with you?

Then say: I refuse to die an unlived life! You beat out 40 million sperm to get here, and you'll never have to face such odds again. Walk through the field of life and leave a trail behind.

One day, one of my rich friends brought my mother a new pair of shoes for me. Now, even though we weren't well off, I didn't want them; they were a size nine and I was a size nine and a half. My mother didn't listen and told my sister to go get some Vaseline, which she rubbed all over my feet. Then my mother had me put those shoes on, minding that I didn't scrunch down the heel. She had my sister run some water in the bathtub, and I was told to get in and walk around in the water. I said that my feet hurt. She just ignored me and asked about my day at school, how everything went and did I get into any fights? I knew what she was up to, that she was trying to distract me, so I said I had only gotten into three fights. After a while mother asked me if my feet still hurt. I admitted that the pain had indeed lessened. She kept me walking in that tub until I had a brand new pair of comfortable, size nine and a half shoes.

You see, once the leather in the shoes got wet, they stretched! And what you need to do is stretch a little. I believe that most people don't set high goals and miss them, but rather, they set lower goals and hit them and then they stay there, stuck on the side of the highway of life. When you're pursuing your greatness, you don't know what your limitations are, and you need to act like you don't have any. If you shoot for the moon and miss, you'll still be in the stars.

You also need coaching (a mentor). Why? There are times you, too, will find yourself parked on the side of the highway of life with no gas in the vehicle. What you need then is someone to stop and offer to pick up some gas down the road a ways and bring it back to you. That person is your coach. Yes, they are there for advice, but their main job is to help you through the difficulties that life throws at all of us.

Another reason for having a coach is that you can't see the picture when you're in the frame. In other words, he or she can often see where you are with a clarity and focus that's unavailable to you. They're not going to leave you parked along the road of life, nor are they going to allow you to be stuck in the moment like a photo in a frame.

And let's say you just can't see you're way forward. You don't believe it's possible. Sometimes you just have to believe in someone's belief in you. This could be your coach, a loved one or even a staunch friend. You need to hear them say you can do it, time and again. Because, after all, faith comes from hearing and hearing and hearing.

Look at it this way. Most people fail because of possibility blindness. They can't see what lies before them. There are always possibilities. Because of this, your dream is possible. You may fail often. In fact, I want you to say this: I will fail my way to success. Here is why.

I had a TV show that failed. I felt I had to go back to public speaking. I had failed, so I parked my car for ten years. Then I saw Dr. Wayne Dyer was still on PBS and I decided to call them. They said they would love to work with me and asked where I had been. I wasn't as good as I had been ten years before, as I was out of practice, but I still had to get back in the game. I was determined to drive on empty.

Listen to recordings, go to seminars, challenge yourself, and you'll begin to step into your greatness, you'll begin to fill yourself with the energy you need to climb to ever greater heights. Most people never attend a seminar. They won't invest money in books or audio programs. You put yourself in the top 5 percent just by making a different choice than the average person. This is called contrary thinking. It's a concept taken from the financial industry. One considers choosing the exact opposite behaviour of the average person as a way to get better than average results. You don't have to make the contrarian choice, but if you don't have anything to lose by going that road, why not consider the option?

Make your move before you're ready. Walk by faith not by sight and make sure you're happy doing it. If you can't be happy, what else is there? Helen Keller said, "Life is short, eat the dessert first."

What is faith? Many of us think of God when we think of faith. A different viewpoint claims that faith is a firm belief in something for which there is no proof. I would rather think of faith as something that is believed especially with strong conviction. It is this last definition I am referring to when I say walk by faith not by sight. Be happy and go forth with strong conviction that you are destined for greatness.

An important step on your way to greatness is to take the time to detoxify. You've got to look at the people in your life. What are they doing for you? Are they setting a pace that you can follow? If not, whose pace have you adjusted to? If you're the smartest in your group, find a new group.

Are the people in your life pulling you down or lifting you up? You know what to do, right? Banish the negative and stay with the positive; it's that simple. Dr. Norman Vincent Peale once said (when I was in the audience), "You are special. You have greatness within you, and you can do more than you could ever possibly imagine."

He overrode the inner conversations in my mind and reached the heart of me. He set me on fire. This is yet another reason for seeking out the help of a coach or mentor or other new people in your life. They can do what Dr. Peale did for me. They can set your passion free.

How important is it to have the right kind of person/people on your side? There was a study done that determined it takes 16 people saying you can do something to overcome one person who says you can't do something. That's right, one negative, unsupportive person can wipe out the work of 16 other supportive people. The message can't be any clearer than that.

Let's face the cold, hard truth: most people stay in park along the highway of life. They never feel the passion, the love for their fellow man, or for the work they do. They are stuck in the proverbial rut. What's the reason? There are many reasons, but only one common factor: fear — fear of change, fear of failure, fear of success, fear they may not be good enough, fear of competition, even fear of rejection.

"Rejection is a myth," says Jack Canfield, co-author of The Chicken Soup for the Soul series. "It's not like you get a slap in the face each time you are rejected." Why not take every "no" you receive as a vitamin, and every time you take one know you are another step closer to success.

You will win if you don't quit. Even a broken clock is right twice a day.

Professional baseball players, on average, get on base just three times out of every ten times they face the opposing pitcher. Even superstars fail half of the time they appear at the plate.

Top commissioned salespeople face similar odds. They make may make one sale from every three people they see, but it will have taken them between 75 and 100 telephone calls to make the 15 appointments they need to close their five sales for the week. And these are statistics for the elite. Most salespeople never reach these kinds of numbers.

People don't spend their lives working for just one company anymore. This means you must build up a set of skills and experiences that are portable. This can be done a number of ways, but my favourite approaches follow.

You must be willing to do the things others won't do in order to have tomorrow the things that others don't have. Provide more service than you get paid for. Set some high standards for yourself.

Begin each day with your most difficult task. The rest of the day will seem more enjoyable and a whole lot easier.

Someone needs help with a problem? Be the solution to that problem.

Also, find those tasks that are being consistently ignored and do them. You'll be surprised by the results. An acquaintance of mine used this approach at a number of entry-level positions and each time he quickly ended up being offered a position in management.

You must increase your energy. Kick it up a notch. We are spirits having a physical existence; let your spirit shine. Quit frittering away your energy. Use it to move you closer to the achievement of your dreams. Refuse to spend it on non-productive activities.

What do people say about you when you leave a room? Are you willing to take responsibility—to walk your talk. There is a terrible epidemic sweeping our nation, and it is the refusal to take responsibility for one's actions. Consider that at some point in any situation there will have been a moment where you could have done something to change the outcome. To that end you are responsible for what happened. It's a hard thing to accept, but it's true.

Life's hard. It was hard when I was told I had cancer. I had sunken into despair, and was hiding away in my study when my son came in. My son asked me if I was going to die. What could I do? I told him I was going to fight, even though I was scared. I also told him that I needed some help. Not because I was weak but because I wanted to stay strong. Keep asking until you get help. Don't stop until you get it.

A setback is the setup for a comeback. A setback is simply a misstep on the long road of success. It means nothing in the larger scheme of things. And, surprisingly, it sets you up for your next win. It tends to focus you and your energy on your immediate goals, paving the way for your next sprint, for your comeback.

It's worth it. Your dreams are worth the sacrifices you'll have to make to achieve them. Find five reasons that will make your dreams worth it for you. Say to yourself, I refuse to live an unlived life.

If you are casual about your dreams, you'll end up a casualty. You must be passionate about your dreams, living and breathing them throughout your days. You've got to be hungry! People who are hungry refuse to take no for an answer. Make NO your vitamin. Be unstoppable. Be hungry.

Let me give you an example of what I mean by hungry …

I decided I wanted to become a disc jockey, so I went down to the local radio station and asked the manager, Mr. Milton "Butterball" Smith, if he had a job available for a disc jockey. He said he did not. The next day I went back, and Mr. Smith asked "Weren't you here yesterday?" I explained that I was just checking to see if anyone was sick or had died. He responded by telling me not to come back again. Day three, I went back again—with the same story. Mr. Smith told me to get out of there. I came back the fourth day and gave Mr. Smith my story one more time. He was so beside himself that he told me to get him a cup of coffee. I said, "Yes, sir!" That's how I became the errand boy.

While working as an errand boy at the station, I took every opportunity to hang out with the deejays and to observe them working. After I had taught myself how to run the control room, it was just a matter of biding my time.

Then one day an opportunity presented itself. One of the disc jockeys by the name of Rockin' Roger was drinking heavily while he was on the air. It was a Saturday afternoon. And there I was, the only one there.

I watched him through the control-room window. I walked back and forth in front of that window like a cat watching a mouse, saying "Drink, Rock, Drink!" I was young. I was ready. And I was hungry.

Pretty soon, the phone rang. It was the station manager. He said, "Les, this is Mr. Klein."

I said, "Yes, I know."

He said, "Rock can't finish his program."

I said, "Yes sir, I know."

He said, "Would you call one of the other disc jockeys to fill in?"

I said, "Yes sir, I sure will, sir."

And when he hung up, I said, "Now he must think I'm crazy." I called up my mama and my girlfriend, Cassandra, and I told them, "Ya'll go out on the front porch and turn up the radio, I'M ABOUT TO COME ON THE AIR!"

I waited 15 or 20 minutes and called the station manager back. I said, "Mr. Klein, I can't find NOBODY!"

He said, "Young boy, do you know how to work the controls?"

I said, "Yes, sir."

He said, "Go in there, but don't say anything. Hear me?"

I said, "Yes, sir."

I couldn't wait to get old Rock out of the way. I went in there, took my seat behind that turntable, flipped on the microphone and let 'er rip.

"Look out, this is me, LB., triple P. Les Brown your platter-playin' papa. There were none before me and there will be none after me, therefore that makes me the one and only. Young and single and love to mingle, certified, bona fide and indubitably qualified to bring you satisfaction and a whole lot of action. Look out baby, I'm your LOVE man."

I WAS HUNGRY!

During my adult life I've been a deejay, a radio station manager, a Democrat in the Ohio Legislature, a minister, a TV personality, an author and a public speaker, but I've always looked after what I valued most—my mother. What I want for her is one of my dreams, one of my goals.

My life has been a true testament to the power of positive thinking and the infinite human potential. I was born in an abandoned building on a floor in Liberty City, a low-income section of Miami, Florida, and adopted at six weeks of age by Mrs. Mamie Brown, a 38-year-old single woman, cafeteria cook and domestic worker. She had very little education or financial means, but a very big heart and the desire to care for myself and my twin brother. I call myself Mrs. Mamie Brown's Baby Boy and I say that all that I am and all that I ever hoped to be, I owe to my mother.

My determination and persistence in searching for ways to help my mother overcome poverty and developing my philosophy to do whatever it takes to achieve success led me to become a distinguished authority on harnessing human potential and success. That philosophy is best expressed by the following …

> "If you want a thing bad enough to go out and fight for it,
> to work day and night for it,
> to give up your time, your peace and your sleep for it…
> if all that you dream and scheme is about it,
> and life seems useless and worthless without it…
> if you gladly sweat for it and fret for it and plan for it
> and lose all your terror of the opposition for it…
> if you simply go after that thing you want
> with all of your capacity, strength and sagacity,
> faith, hope and confidence and stern pertinacity…
> if neither cold, poverty, famine, nor gout,
> sickness nor pain, of body and brain,
> can keep you away from the thing that you want…
> if dogged and grim you beseech and beset it,
> with the help of God, you will get it!"

Branding Small Business

RAYMOND AARON

B randing is an incredibly important tool for creating and building your business. Large companies have been benefiting from branding ever since people first started selling things to other people. Branding made those businesses big.

If you're a small business owner, you probably imagine that small companies are different and don't need branding as much as large companies do. Not true. The truth is small businesses need branding just as much, if not more, than large companies.

Perhaps you've thought about branding, but assumed you'd need millions of dollars to do it properly, or that branding is just the same thing as marketing. Nothing could be further from the truth.

Marketing is the engine of your company's success. Branding is the fuel in that engine.

In the old days, salespeople were a big part of the selling process. They recommended one product over another and laid out the reasons why it was better. Salespeople had credibility because they knew about all the products, and customers often took the advice they had to offer.

Today, consumers control the buying process. They shop in big box stores, super-sized supermarkets, and over the Internet — where there are no salespeople. Buyers now get online and gather information beforehand. They learn about all the products available and look to see if there really is any difference between them. Consumers also read reviews and check social media to see if both the company and the product are reputable. In other words, they want to know what the brand is all about.

The way of commerce used to be: "Nothing happens till something is sold." Today it's: "Nothing happens till something is branded!"

DEFINING A BRAND

A brand is a proper name that stands for something. It lives in the consumer's mind, has positive or negative characteristics, and invokes a feeling or an image. In short, it's a person's perception of a product or a company.

When all goes well, consumers associate the same characteristics with a brand that the company talks about in its advertising, public relations, marketing and sales materials. Of course, when a product doesn't live up to what the company says about it, the brand gets a bad reputation. On the other hand, if a product or service over-delivers on the promises made, the brand can become a superstar.

RECOGNIZING BRANDING AND ITS CHARACTERISTICS

Branding is the science and art of making something that isn't unique, unique. Branding in the marketplace is the same as branding on a ranch. On a ranch, ranchers use branding to differentiate their cattle from every other rancher's cattle (because all cattle look pretty much the same). In the marketplace, branding is what makes a product stand out in a crowd of similar products. The right branding gets you noticed, remembered and sold — or perhaps I should say bought, because today it is all about buying, not selling.

There are four main characteristics of branding that make it an integral part of the marketing and purchasing process.

1. Branding makes you trustworthy and known

Branding makes a product more special than other products. With branding, a normal, everyday product has a personality, and a first and last name, and people know who you are.

In today's marketplace, most products are, more or less, just like their competition. Toilet paper is toilet paper, milk is milk, and a grocery store by any other name is still a grocery store. However, branding takes a product and makes it unique. For example, high-quality drinking water is available from just about every tap in the Western world and it's free, but people pay good money for it when it comes in a bottle. Branding takes bottled water and makes Evian.

Furthermore, every aspect of your brand gives potential customers a feeling or comfort level that they associate with you. The more powerful and positive that feeling is, the more easily and more frequently they will want to do business with you and, indeed, will do business with you.

2. Branding differentiates you from others

Strong branding makes you better than your competition, and makes your product name memorable and easy to remember. Even if your product is absolutely the same as every other product like it, branding makes it special. Branding makes it the first product a consumer thinks about when deciding to make a purchase.

Branding also makes a product seem popular. Everyone knows about it, which implicitly says people like it. And, if people like it, it must be good.

3. Branding makes you worth more money

The stronger your branding is, the more likely people are willing to spend that little bit extra because they believe you, your product, your service, or your business are worth it. They may say they won't, but they will. They do it all the time.

For example, a one-pound box of Godiva chocolates costs about $40; the same weight of Hershey's Kisses costs about $4. The quality of the chocolate isn't ten times greater. The reason people buy Godiva is that the brand Godiva means "gift" whereas the brand Hershey means "snack". Gifts obviously cost more than snacks.

4. Branding pre-sells your product

In the buying age, people most often make the decision on which products to pick up before they walk into the store. The stronger the branding, the more likely people are to think in terms of your product rather than the product category. For example, people are as likely, maybe even more likely, to add Hellmann's to the shopping list as they are to write down simply mayo. The same is true for soda, ketchup, and many other products with successful, strong branding.

Plus, as soon as a shopper gets to the shelf, branding can provide a quick reminder of what products to grab in a few ways:

- An icon or logo
- A specific color
- An audio icon

BRANDING IN A SMALL BUSINESS

Big companies spend millions of dollars on advertising, marketing, and public relations (PR) to build recognition of a new product name. They get their selling messages out to the public using television, radio, magazines, and the Internet. They can even throw money at damage control when necessary. The strategies for branding are the same in a small business, but the scale, costs, and a few of the tactics change.

Make your brand name work harder

The name of a small business can mean everything in terms of branding. Your brand name needs to work harder for your business than you do. It's the first thing a prospective customer sees, and it is how they will remember you. A brand name has to be memorable when spoken, and focused in its meaning. If the name doesn't represent what consumers believe about a product and the company that makes it, then that brand will fail.

In building your product's reputation and image, less is often significantly more. Make sure the name you choose immediately gives a sense of what you do.

Large corporations have millions of dollars to take a meaningless brand name and make it stand for something. Small businesses don't, so use words that really mean something. Strive for something interesting and be right on point. You don't need to be boring.

Plumbers, for example, would do well setting themselves apart with names like "The On-Time Plumber" or "24/7 Plumbing". The same is true for electricians, IT providers, or even marketing consultants. Plenty of other types of business are so general in nature they just don't work hard enough in a business or product name.

Even the playing field: The Net

The Internet has leveled the playing field for small businesses like nothing else. You can use the Internet in several ways to market your brand:

Website: Developing and maintaining a website is easier than ever. Anyone can find your business regardless of its size.

Social Media: Facebook and Twitter can promote your brand in a cost-effective manner.

BUILDING YOUR BRAND WITH THE BRANDING LADDER

Even if you do everything perfectly the first time (and I don't know anyone who does), branding takes time. How much time isn't just up to you, but you can speed things along by understanding the different levels of branding, as well as the business and marketing strategies that can get you to the top.

Introducing the Branding Ladder

Moving through the levels of branding is like climbing a ladder to the top of the marketplace. The Branding Ladder has five distinct rungs and, unlike stairs, you can't take them two at a time. You have to take them in order, and some businesses spend more time on each rung than others.

You can also think of the Branding Ladder in terms of a scale from zero to ten. Everyone starts at zero. If you properly climb the ladder, you can end up at 12 out of 10. The Branding Ladder below shows a special rung at the top of the ladder that can take your business over the top. The following section explains the Branding Ladder and how your small business can move up it.

THE BRANDING LADDER	
Brand Advocacy	12/10
Brand Insistence	10/10
Brand Preference	3/10
Brand Awareness	1/10
Brand Absence	0/10

Rung 1: Living in the void

Your business, in fact every business, starts at the bottom rung, which is called brand absence, meaning you have no brand whatsoever except your own name. On a scale of one to ten, brand absence is, of course, zero. That's the worst place to live and obviously the most difficult entrepreneurially. The good news is that the only way is up.

Ninety-seven percent of businesses live on this rung of the Branding Ladder. They earn far less than they want to earn, far less than they should earn, and far less than they would earn if they did exactly the same work under a real brand.

Rung 2: Achieving awareness

Brand awareness is a good first step up the ladder to the second rung. Actually, it's really good, especially because 97 percent of businesses never get there. You want people to be aware of you. When person A speaks to person B and says, "Have you heard of "The 24/7 Plumber?" You want the answer to be "yes".

On that scale of one to ten, however, brand awareness is only a one. It's better than nothing, but not that much better. Although people know of your brand, being aware doesn't mean that they are interested in buying it. Coca Cola drinkers know about Pepsi, but they don't drink it.

Rung 3: Becoming the preferred brand

Getting to the third rung, brand preference, is definitely a real step up. This rung means that people prefer to use your product or service rather than that of your competition. They believe there is a real difference between you and others, and you're their first choice. This rung is a crucial branding stage for parity products, such as bottled water and breakfast cereals, not to mention plumbers, electricians, lawyers, and all the others. Brand preference is clearly better than brand awareness, but it's less than halfway up the ladder.

Car rental companies represent a perfect example of why brand preference may not be enough. When someone lands at an airport and needs to rent a car on the spot, he or she may go straight to the preferred rental counter. If that company has a car available, it's a sale. However, if all the cars for that company have been rented, the person will move to the next rental kiosk without much thought, because one rental car is just as good as another.

Exerting Brand Preference needs to be easy and convenient

If all you have is brand preference, your business is on shaky ground and you can lose business for the feeblest of reasons. Very few people go to a second or third supermarket just to find their favorite brand of bottled water. Similarly, a shopper may prefer one store over another but, if both stores sell the same products, he or she will often go to the closest store even if it is not the better liked one. The reason for staying nearby does not need to be a dramatic one — the shopper may simply be tired, on a tight schedule, or not in the mood to travel.

Rung 4: Making it you and only you

When your customers are so committed to your product or service that they won't accept a substitute, you have reached the fourth rung of the Branding Ladder. All companies strive to reach this place, called brand insistence.

Brand insistence means that someone's experience with a product in terms of performance, durability, customer service, and image has been sufficiently exceptional. As a result, the product has earned an incredible level of loyalty. If the product isn't available where the customer is, he or she will literally not buy something else. Rather, the person will look for the preferred product elsewhere. Can you imagine what a fabulous place this is for a company to be? Brand insistence is the best of the best, the perfect ten out of ten, the whole ball of wax.

Apple is a perfect example of brand insistence

Apple users don't just think, they know in their heads and hearts, that anything made by Apple is technologically-advanced, user-friendly, and just all-around superior. Committed to everything Apple, Mac users won't even entertain the thought that a PC may have positive attributes.

Apple people love everything about their Macs, iPads, iPhones, the Mac stores and all those apps. When the company introduces a new product, many of its brand-insistent fans actually wait in line overnight to be one of the first to have it. Steve Jobs is one of their idols.

Considering one big potential problem

Unfortunately, you can lose brand insistence much more quickly than you can achieve it. Brand-insistent customers have such high expectations that they can be disillusioned or disappointed by just one bad product experience. You also have to consistently reinforce the positives because insistence can fade over time. Even someone who has bought and re-bought a specific brand of car for the last 20 years can decide it's just time for a change. That's how fickle the world is.

At ten out of ten, brand insistence may seem like the top rung of the ladder, but it's not. One rung is actually better, and it involves getting your brand-insistent customers to keep polishing your brand for you.

Rung 5: Getting customers to do the work for you

Brand advocacy is the highest rung on the ladder. It's better than ten out of ten because you have customers who are so happy with your product that they want everyone to know about it and use it. Think of them as uber-fans. Not only do they recommend you to friends and family, they also practically shout your praises from the rooftops, interrupt conversations among strangers to give their opinion, and tell everyone they meet how fantastic you are. Most companies can only aspire to this level of customer satisfaction. Apple is one of the few large corporations in recent history that has brand advocates all over the world.

- Brand advocacy does the following five extraordinary things for your company. Brand advocacy:

- Provides a level of visibility that you couldn't pay for if you tried. Brand advocates are so enthusiastic they talk about you all the time, and reach people in ways general media and public relations can't. You get great visibility because they make sure people actually listen.

- Delivers free advertising and public relations. Companies love the extra super-positive messaging, all for free.

- Affords a level of credibility that literally can't be bought. Brand advocates are more than just walking testimonials. They are living proof that you are the best.

- Provides pre-sold prospective customers. Advocate recommendations carry so much weight that they are worth much more than plain referrals. They deliver customers ready and committed to purchasing your product or service.

- Increases profits exponentially. Brand advocates are money-making machines for your business because they increase sales and decrease marketing costs.

For these reasons, brand advocacy is 12 out of 10!!

BRANDING YOURSELF: HOW TO DO SO IN FOUR EASY WAYS

If you're interested in branding your product or company, you may not be sure where to begin. The good news: I'm here to help. You can brand in many ways, but here I pare it down to four ways to help you start:

Branding by association

This way involves hanging out with and being seen with people who are very much higher than you in your particular niche.

Branding by achievement

This way repurposes your previous achievements.

Branding by testimonial

This way makes use of the testimonials that you receive but have likely never used.

Branding by WOW

A WOW is the pleasantly unexpected, the equivalent of going the extra mile. The easiest and most certain way to WOW people is to tell them that you've written a book. To discover how you can write a book of own, go to www.BrandingSmallBusinessForDummies.com.

Sex, Love and Relationships

DR. JOHN GRAY

Just as great sex is important to lasting love, good health is important to sex and relationships. About 12 years ago, I cured myself of early stage Parkinson's disease. The doctors were amazed, but my wife was even more amazed. She noted that our relationship and sex life had become dramatically better. It turns out that the natural supplements I used to reverse Parkinson's can also make you more attentive and loving in your relationship. At that point, I realized that good relationship skills alone were not enough to sustain love and passion for a lifetime.

I shared many insights gained from my 40 years' experience as a marriage counselor and coach in *Men Are From Mars, Women Are From Venus*. And while my insights go a long way towards helping men and women understand and support each other, good communication skills alone are not always enough. For better relationships, we not only need to be healthy, but we must also experience optimum brain function.

If you are tired, depressed, anxious, not sleeping well, or in pain, then certainly romantic feelings will become a thing of the past. My recovery from Parkinson's revealed to me the profound connection between the quality of our health and our relationships. This insight has motivated me, over the past twelve years, to research the secrets of optimum health as a foundation for lasting love.

These are health secrets that are generally not explored in medical school. In medical school, doctors are indoctrinated into the culture of examining the symptoms, identifying the sickness, and prescribing a drug to treat that sickness. They learn very little about how to be healthy or to sustain successful relationships.

There are no university courses entitled "Better Nutrition For Better Sex". Drugs sometimes save lives, but they also have negative side effects that do little to preserve the passion in a relationship. Ideally, drugs should be used as a last resort and 90 % of our health plan should be drug free. From this perspective, the heath care crisis, as well as our high rate of divorce in America, is indirectly caused by our dependence on doctors and prescription drugs.

Most people have not even considered that taking prescribed drugs (even for the small stuff) can weaken their relationships, which in turn makes them more vulnerable to more disease. For example, if you are feeling depressed or anxious, a drug may numb your pain, but it does nothing to help you correct the cause of your problem. It can even prevent you from feeling your natural motivation to get the emotional support you need. In a variety of ways, our common health complaints are all expressions of two major conditions: our lack of education to identify and support unmet gender-specific emotional needs; and our lack of education to identify and support unmet gender-specific nutritional needs.

With an understanding of natural solutions that have been around for thousands of years, drugs are not needed to treat many common complaints. Some symptoms like low energy, weight gain, allergies, hormonal imbalance, mood swings, poor sleep, indigestion, lack of focus, ADD and ADHD, procrastination, low motivation, memory loss, decreased libido, PMS, vaginal dryness, muscle and joint pain, or the lack of passion in life and/or our relationships can be treated drug-free. By using drugs (even over-the-counter drugs) to treat these common complaints, our bodies and relationships are weakened, making us more vulnerable to bigger and more costly health challenges like cancer, diabetes, heart disease, auto-immune disease, dementia, and Alzheimer's. In simple terms, by handling the easy stuff (the common complaints) without doctors and drugs, we can protect ourselves from the big stuff (cancer, heart disease, dementia, etc.) We can be healthy and also enjoy lasting love and passion in our personal lives.

Even if you are taking anti-depressants or hormone replacement therapy, sometimes all it takes to stop treating the symptom is to directly handle the cause. With specific mineral orotates (something most people have never heard of) or omega three oil from the brains of salmon, your stress levels immediately drop and you begin to feel happy and in love again.

For every health challenge, we have explored the effects on our relationships, with as well as natural remedies that can sometimes produce immediate positive results. You can find these natural solutions to common health complaints for free at my website: www.MarsVenus.com.

What they don't teach in medical school is how to be healthy and happy without the use of drugs or hormone replacement. By refusing drugs and taking responsibility for your health, a wealth of new possibilities can become available to you. We are designed to be healthy and happy, and it is within our reach if we commit to increasing our knowledge.

New research regarding the brain differences in men and women reveals how specific nutritional supplements, combined with gender-specific relationship and self-nurturing skills, can stimulate the hormones of health, happiness and increased energy. Over the past 10 years in my healing center in California, I witnessed how natural solutions coupled with gender-specific relationship skills could solve our common health complaints without drugs. By addressing these common complaints without prescribed drugs, not only do we feel better, but our relationships have the potential to improve dramatically.

Ultimately the cause of all our common complaints is higher stress levels. Researchers around the world all agree that chronic stress levels in our bodies provide a basis for any and all disease to take hold. An easy and quick solution for lowering our stress reactions is specific nutritional support combined with gender-smart relationship skills. Extra nutritional support is needed because stress depletes the body very quickly of essential nutrients. When a car engine is running more quickly, it uses fuel more quickly. When we are stressed, we need both extra nutrients and extra emotional support. Understanding what we need to take and where to get it requires education. Every week day at www.MarsVenus.com I have a live daily show where I freely answer questions and provide this much-needed new gender-specific insight.

At www.MarsVenus.com, we are happy to share what we have learned for creating healthy bodies and positive relationships. You can find a host of natural solutions for common complaints and feel confident that you have the power to feel fully alive with an abundance of energy and positive feelings that will enrich all your relationships.

Never Give Up!

My Journey to Purpose

VIVIAN STARK

NEVER GIVE UP: GROWTH AND SUCCESS COME IN INCREMENTS, NOT LEAPS

My desire is to encourage you with my life story. I have spent my life learning and improving myself, and I am thrilled to share what I have learned with you. Today I am living my definition of success. I have said NO TO THE PITY PARTY! Personal growth and development are a daily diet staple, and have fueled me in my business and entrepreneurial successes.

I wake up every day, knowing I am living my life with purpose, knowing I am the kind of person I always wanted to be. I have faced many challenges; my story has failures as well as successes. But I have learned that setbacks are only a part of the story; they are not the whole story. The story keeps going as long as you keep trying. You can choose to quit and make the story end in failure or dissatisfaction, or you can choose to keep trying and make your story what you want it to be.

Never give up. Success and growth do not come in leaps, they come in increments. The challenges will keep coming at you and sometimes it feels like two steps forward, one step back. But remember you did have those steps forward and you will again – if you never give up. You can choose to be overcome by dreck that life throws at you, or you can open your eyes to the love and opportunity that are always there too. You can have the life you want if you never, never, never give up on what is important – You.

IT IS YOUR LIFE - LIVE IT YOUR WAY

My life is my own for the making, but I did not always know this. I lived a very sheltered life as a child, fiercely protected by my overbearing Greek parents. I was not allowed to do the 'normal' girl things, like have sleepovers or join the Girl Guides to be a Brownie. When I was older I was not allowed to date for fear of gossip within my community. My parents lived in fear of the unknown. I lived in fear of being reprimanded if I disobeyed.

Despite my fear, insecurity, and extremely introverted personality, I pushed myself to exert my independence and fulfill certain goals that I set out for myself. From a very young age, I felt that I always needed to prove myself. To prove that I was pretty enough, smart enough, or even good enough. I worked tirelessly to achieve my dreams, never sharing them with anyone for fear of being ridiculed.

I began pursuing my goals as a young teen who wanted to fit in. I lived in an affluent area of Vancouver and always felt out of place. I did not have all the cool clothes that everyone else had, so I worked with my brother as a gardener cutting grass for one of my dad's clients. I saved my money and bought the clothes I wanted so that I would 'fit in' with the crowd. Despite this, I never felt that I fit in with other kids.

I was a rather "ugly duckling" as a younger girl, with a massive overbite and awkward shyness about me. After having braces, I felt my "ugly" stage was behind me and I decided to take a modeling class over several weeks one summer when I was in high school. My parents did not support me in this decision, so I chose to pay for it myself. The modeling class cost $800. I worked at Zellers for $3.00/hour. I persevered and saved enough money to pay for the class.

It turns out that the modeling class was just what I needed. I learned how to carry myself and exude confidence. After finishing the class, I took several modeling jobs and had many successes in my short modeling career. I made the cover of the then prestigious Back to School catalog for Eaton's Department Store, along with several other fun and exciting modeling adventures.

My modeling highlight and a fond memory was when I was hired for a ski catalog. (They wanted a curvy model. Who knew that sometimes it pays to not be super skinny!) We were taken up to the top of Blackcomb Mountain by helicopter before the official ski season opening. I remember having to jump out of the helicopter into three feet of snow because the helipad was snow-covered, and the helicopter could not land. I was paid $850 per day for three days. It was a dream come true. I felt validated.

When I was nineteen I began dating a handsome Greek guy I met at a wedding. Before I knew it, his parents and my parents got together and began planning our wedding. I literally cannot remember him actually asking me to marry him. How sad is that? Some time before our wedding I found out that he was into drugs and was still seeing his ex-girlfriend. I broke up with him and cancelled the wedding.

To escape well-meaning friends and relatives, I took an extended holiday to Greece where I could recover from the breakup. Armed with my modeling composite cards and my lovely, fashionable clothes, I hoped to land some modeling jobs while I was there. Instead, I met another handsome Greek guy who was smooth and charming. He swept me off my feet.

In classic old-school Greek fashion, my mom flew to Greece to check him out and determine whether he was a suitable partner for me. Like I said, I lived a sheltered life. She approved and, after a civil wedding in Canada, I moved to Greece to start my life with my new husband.

The first thing he did when we settled in to our home was give away all my beloved clothes. He proceeded to tell me what I could and could not do, where I could and could not go, and how I had to act. He, like my parents, was consumed with what other people thought of him and now me. I was terrified. What had I done?

I realized very quickly I had made a huge mistake and wanted to leave him and go back to Canada. To my surprise, I was already pregnant. Too embarrassed to tell anyone my sad state of affairs, I stayed in Greece. I had made an agreement with my husband that our children would be born in Canada. I did not want to risk my children having to go to the army if they were boys. After my first son was born, I returned to Greece.

When I became pregnant with my second son, I decided to leave Greece, not to return. I told my husband I was going back to Canada and he could come with me or not. He chose to move to Canada with me, but we broke up after a few years. Our marriage was just not meant to be, but I was blessed with two healthy, adorable and rambunctious boys that I loved so much.

Once divorced, my husband went back to Greece to avoid paying child support and to be near his momma, so she could pamper and take care of him. (It's a Greek thing. He was a huge momma's boy. Never again.) I was determined that my two boys would never be momma's boys!

THE SETBACK IS NOT THE END OF THE STORY
PUSH YOURSELF TO YOUR NEXT GREAT CHAPTER

For the next few years, I lived in low-income housing while raising my boys and working at Woodward's department store. Then, I left my job at Woodward's and began a career in banking. I started out on the front lines working as a teller. After six weeks I was promoted to the prestigious side counter position. Within a year I was promoted again to managing tens of millions of dollars of lawyers' trust funds in an exclusive, independent position.

I was always pushing myself to be better, to do more, be more, have more so I could give more. I wanted to improve myself and my income to support my family. I had an internal drive to never give up. I wanted to prove everyone wrong. I would make it. I could do this! During these years I learned to appreciate life's lessons and gifts and I continued to grow.

Ten years after my first marriage, I married a second time. I became pregnant soon after our wedding in Hawaii but spent most of my time during our marriage being neglected by my husband. As soon as my daughter was born, I no longer existed in his eyes. I later found out that my husband had a girlfriend before, during, and after our entire marriage. He worked with her; she was married, too, and the four of us occasionally hung out together as couples. Needless to say, the marriage did not last, but I would not change a thing as I have my beautiful daughter from that relationship.

I spent the next years relentlessly trying to find my passion. I worked in banking, direct sales, office supplies, a genealogical search company, and as a sales manager for a roofing distribution company. I also went to night school while working full-time and raising my kids, to get my diploma in International Trade. Additionally, I began a calling card company in Santiago, Chile that I launched at the Canada/Chile Trade Mission in 2003.

OPPORTUNITY KEEPS KNOCKING, SO OPEN THE DOOR!

I was very proud of the calling card company. It was a crazy dream, but I wanted to make it happen. Recognizing a huge opportunity, I wanted to offer an affordable service that we took for granted in Canada. The large telecommunications companies had a very different view on my entry to the marketplace and I was forced out of business when they pressured my distribution channel to drop me. Unfortunately, my venture was short-lived after significant effort and money had been invested. I planned to travel back to Chile to negotiate a deal with another distributor when I was rear-ended in a car accident and suffered severe whiplash, leaving me unable to travel. I had to move on from this company but by this time I knew it was not the end. I knew other opportunities would come my way.

By 2007, I was working for a computer company selling proprietary software and hardware for restaurants. My expertise in sales and customer service had grown significantly by then. I had come a long way from the introverted little Greek girl who thought she was not good enough. With perseverance, training, and a belief in myself I had become a great salesperson.

I loved working with customers and was enjoying my new career when I began having severe migraines regularly. I was also having issues with my sinuses. I thought I probably had a severe sinus infection, but my nose and upper gums were numb, which was troubling.

That August was one big headache, literally. I had eight migraines that month and each one put me down for two to five days. I went to the doctor and had several tests run, including a CT scan. After the CT scan doctors finally determined the cause of my sinus trouble and migraines.

I will never forget that day. The doctor's office called and scheduled me for a 7:00 PM appointment. The doctor came in and told me that I had a brain tumor and that she was very sorry, but she did not know whether it was benign or malignant. She had not consulted a neurologist before meeting with me. I drove home in a state of shock and called my mom to tell her the news.

I learned that I had a meningioma, a benign brain tumor. After an MRI, I learned it measured 3.3 x 3.4 x 4.4 cm, was in my right frontal lobe, and had probably been growing for twenty or thirty years. Only recently had it grown large enough to begin causing migraines, sinus pain, and facial numbness.

Within a month I would be having major brain surgery to remove the tumor. Oddly enough, I was not scared until the day of the surgery, when it really sunk in. I had been told that the tumor was in an excellent location for surgery and that I would not need chemo or radiation afterwards. The tumor was not going to kill me. But with any surgery there is always a risk.

I do not remember much that happened the first week or so post-surgery. When I really came around and began noticing things, the first thing that caught my attention was that I was having significant vision problems. The brain surgeon had touched a nerve in my right eye, causing fourth nerve palsy. I always had this weird talent to do crazy thing with my eyes and move them independently, but this was something I could not control. I had severe double vision. I could only see straight when I looked through a very narrow view if I tilted my chin down. And I could not look to my left at all. When I tried, I lost all focus and control of my eyes.

This condition is similar to a child having a wandering eye. Actually, I had to be seen at Vancouver Children's Hospital to have my condition monitored. This was a very challenging time for me. It was one of the worst times of my life. I had so much stress and anxiety wondering if my vision would be like this forever. My head was permanently disfigured, leaving my self-esteem at an all-time low. My jaw was so stiff from surgery that I could barely open my mouth to eat. I was house-bound, and unable to walk up or down stairs without assistance. I could not read or watch TV to occupy myself because I was constantly dizzy. Every negative thought you could possibly imagine ran through my mind thousands of times each day. I wish I had known then what I know now about keeping a positive mindset, the healing powers of affirmations, an attitude of gratitude, and the law of attraction.

I cannot stress enough how important it is to reach out to family and friends to help you during a medical crisis (or any crisis, for that matter). Having people who love you to support you is so important. Being the independent person that I am, I did not ask for much help. Silly me. Stupid me, actually. I did not want to worry my kids any more than they already were. My mother was such an angel. She lived nearby and prepared meals for us, but for the most part, I was alone in my thoughts in a very dark place.

About five weeks into my recovery, I met someone online. Bored out of my mind, I had gone on a dating site, half-blind, looking for strangers to converse with me. Talk about being desperate! For our first meeting, I rode the bus to downtown Vancouver where we met for a drink. He must have thought I was rather forward on a first date when I grabbed his arm to walk up a few stairs. Little did he know that I grabbed his arm so that I would not fall flat on my face.

We hit it off and developed a relationship. He picked me up every day for several weeks and took me out on his random errands just to get me out of the house. Sometimes we would just hang out. At first, I only told him that I'd had a recent eye surgery. Eventually I told him the extent of the surgery. He was also having some challenges in his life, so it was wonderful to be able to help each other. I cannot tell you what a godsend he was for me. He came into my life exactly when I needed him, and I am forever grateful for what he did for me.

Worried about losing my job, I returned to work twelve weeks post-surgery. I was worried about paying my bills and the mortgage on the house I had recently purchased. I needed the money, or so I thought. In hindsight, that was the worst decision I could have made. I suffered with migraines and vision issues for several weeks before the universe decided I'd had enough. All of the senior managers, including me, were laid off from our jobs. It was the biggest blessing.

I did not work for two years. It was a very trying time. The line of credit was on a steady increase as the months went by, but I needed to heal. My vision took over a year to somewhat normalize, and the severe numbness in my face post surgery lasted for several years.

During this period, I had a lot of time to think. My surgery was a life-changing experience. I could have died. I decided to take on a totally different view on life from this time forward. From this point on, any time an opportunity presented itself I was going to take it.

DEFINE YOUR WORK AND WHAT YOU NEED

Knowing that after all my health problems I would need a job that allowed me to make my health a priority, I decided to choose a job that would work for me rather than choosing to work for the job. I started slowly by taking a 100% sales commission, part-time position that allowed me to work as much or as little as I wanted.

I told my bosses about my medical condition, and that I was not sure how I would respond to being back to work. My boss told me that as long as I was meeting or exceeding my quotas that he would not micromanage me. I would be allowed to do my own thing, which was perfect for me. For some this would be a scary venture to undertake, but I was up for the challenge.

I pushed myself by working long hours, often answering customer emails at 6:00 AM before I went to work and again well into the evening. I needed to build up my customer base and wanted to ensure they were well taken care of. Within less than six months I was working full-time and making a full-time income. I was back!

After working for this company for about four years, a couple of millennials were hired into the mix, and that changed everything for me. I was working independently with little interaction with my bosses for the most part and the millennials were cc'ing him on every email they sent. This is when my interest in generational differences in the workplace was first piqued.

Although I enjoyed the work and my co-workers, my bosses were a different story. My work environment left much to be desired. Receiving year-end bonuses based on sales is a standard practice in the world of sales. When I did not receive a bonus at the end of 2013 because my boss said I was "already making too much money," I decided to look at other business opportunities. Forever the entrepreneur!

I continued working my sales job while seeking other opportunities. I joined an Australian direct sales company and quickly rose to the top of their company, becoming one of their top 20 earners out of 20,000 consultants. I had 1,700 consultants on my team and was the only director in North America. I earned free trips to Australia, Dubai, Aruba, Florence, Manchester, Dallas, and Los Angeles. I finally left my sales job in 2016 to pursue my new business venture full-time.

DREAM BIG AND HELP OTHERS DREAM TOO

I LOVED working with my team. Coaching and mentoring were my passion. In October 2016, I attended a One Day to Greatness seminar with Jack Canfield in Kamloops, BC. After a brief conversation with Jack, I decided to take his Train the Trainer course to become a certified Success Principles Trainer. The intention was to share this new knowledge with my team. I had found purpose and passion in supporting others to build successful teams. I felt fulfilled when I saw their self-esteem and confidence grow. They were conquering their fears and winning!

Unfortunately, I had to resign from the direct sales company in February 2017 when they started having issues with production and delivery. Later that year the company declared bankruptcy. I went through a lot of stress, anxiety, and loss of sleep. Panic attacks became the daily norm for me. I had known the CEO for over eighteen years and was completely in the dark about the state of the company. My team was upset and blaming me. I received a constant stream of Facebook messages and harassing emails. The downfall of the company was out of my control, so I had to bow out. But this was not my first time at the rodeo. I knew that my story did not stop here if I chose to keep trying.

I met someone in late 2016 who introduced me to an opportunity to speak and train businesses on generational differences in the workplace. I was fascinated by this as I saw the struggles my own millennial children were having at work. I look back now at the communication challenges that existed in my previous jobs and wish I knew then how the different generations think and process information. I wanted to more closely understand their environment and what I could do to help. It made perfect sense that bridging the generation gap would improve productivity, communication, collaboration, and make for a happier, more cohesive work environment.

I now know that the behaviors, attitudes, beliefs, experiences, and influences during an individual's formative years really shape who they are and how they behave in all areas of their lives. I was excited about my new-found knowledge, and planned to launch my speaking business by mid-2017.

I hired an image consultant to come to my home and do a complete wardrobe change to prepare me for my speaking career. Having someone go through my wardrobe and tell me to get rid of most of it was a very difficult experience. There were a few tears. I must have attachment issues! I eventually embraced the change and spent thousands of dollars on a new wardrobe to complete my new look.

Then, as luck would have it, I broke a veneer on my front tooth. No big deal, I thought. I had been through this before and would just have it replaced.

This was the beginning of my dental nightmare. From May 31, 2017 through December 21, 2017, I had twenty-six dental appointments to fix my front tooth. I began lisping and developed what doctors believe is a stress-related condition. I lost the saliva in my mouth, had burning in my throat from acid reflux brought on by stress, my voice was constantly hoarse, and I spent several months waking up with panic attacks. I never knew from one to day to the next if I would have a voice or not, so I had to put everything on hold.

I saw every doctor and specialist I believed might be able to help me. I was taking six pills a day to help with my various symptoms. I hated this! I needed to feel better; I needed to heal my body naturally. I would not stop until I got the answers I needed. I moved away from traditional medicine, stopped taking all my medications, and began incorporating EFT (Emotional Freedom Technique), also known as Tapping, Reiki, and Bioenergy work, to heal my body.

Eventually, my body and voice were getting to the point where I could speak relatively well, I decided to move forward with the training business. I hired a business coach to get me on the right track, mentally and physically. He helped me tremendously during a very difficult time. I also attended Raymond Aaron's Speaker and Communication Workshop, which totally changed my training and speaking style. It gave me the confidence I was lacking and sent me on a whole new trajectory for my business. I began my own company, Gen-Connect Training in early 2018. It has been an amazing ride. I am much more at peace and ready for the next stage in my life.

LIVING IN THE POSITIVE HAS MADE MY LIFE

Although I have been blessed with many struggles, I have also enjoyed many successes. I have experienced relationships that did not work out, work and business challenges, worries when raising three children as a single parent, medical challenges, and many dreams and goals that seemed impossible. The one thing I always knew for sure was that if I gave up and wallowed in self-pity, I would be letting myself and my children down. That was not an option. Success was the only acceptable outcome.

I wanted to show my children what a strong, self-sufficient and resourceful mother I could be, and that they could always rely on me. I wanted to set an example and prove to myself and my children that I could provide for us no matter what. I am very proud of the amazing people my children have become; they are strong, independent, kind, respectful, and loving. This is the true meaning of success for me. Out of all the things I have accomplished thus far, they are my crowning glory.

FIVE STRATEGIES FOR A SUCCESSFUL LIFE

1) **Always have a positive mindset.** This is a crucial component. Before you get into the power of a positive mindset and the law of attraction, spend some time listening to what you are currently telling yourself. Check in with yourself. What is going on with you? We constantly speak to ourselves with an inner voice which is sometimes quietly whispering and sometimes yelling. Once you have spent a few days noticing how you speak to yourself, you may not like it very much; after all, you are your own worst critic. Be accountable for how you speak to yourself. Never fear, you have the power to change that inner voice!

Do you believe you are the product of everything that has happened to you in your life? Your inner voice may try to convince you that you are a victim of your circumstances and your past. Reflect and acknowledge the things that have happened to you and where you are now. Then prepare to move past them.

2) Shift your mindset using the law of attraction. You can influence things around you so that things happen FOR you rather than TO you. The universal principle of the law of attraction is that 'like attracts like.' The law of attraction manifests through your thoughts by drawing to you not only thoughts and ideas that are alike, but also people who think like you, along with corresponding situations and possibilities. It is the magnetic power of the universe which draws similar energies to each other.

The law of attraction is already working in your life, intentional or not. If you have a negative mindset, many unpleasant or unwanted things are probably happening in your life, and you may see negative things happening all around you. Think back to how you speak to yourself. Be mindful of your thoughts and that inner voice. Begin to think positively.

Along with thinking positively, begin to intentionally think and feel the things that you would like to have in your life. The most common things people desire are love, a career, good relationships, health, and wealth. Visualize a mental image of what you want to achieve. Repeat positive, affirming statements to create and bring into your life what you visualize or repeat in your mind. In other words, use the power of your thoughts and words.

Imagine that what you desire is already a part of your life. Acknowledge it with each of your five senses, to the extent that you can. Spend time imagining your life once you have acquired what it is that you want. Write out your affirmations and read them aloud at least once daily. You will begin to draw them to you when you act as though you already have what it is that you want. Persistence is key!

3) Take calculated risks. Do you encourage yourself to stay where you are and play it safe? Safe can be dangerous. I encourage you to take calculated risks. If you do not try new things you will never know how far you can go. When opportunities present themselves, jump on them. It may be your one and only chance. Push yourself and do not take no for an answer. Keep digging until you find the answer you want.

Quitting is always an option. Well, it is an option for those who are content living a mediocre life. Quitting is an option unless you want to live an amazing life with a purpose. If you want to live the life of your dreams, you must not give up. Do not give up and never stop learning. If you continue to learn, you will continue to grow both personally and professionally.

4) Appreciate all of life's lessons and gifts with an attitude of gratitude. Learn and grow from your failures. Let life's challenges teach you to persevere even when all you want to do is give up. Remind yourself that the only outcome you will accept is success.

5) NEVER Give Up. We all face adversities and challenges in life. It takes character, drive, and a positive mindset to persevere, overcome, and excel in life. The only person who can stop you from achieving your goals is you. If I can do it, so can you. Go for it!

Do you, your team, or organization want to be inspired to change your future and find your purpose?

Do you want to learn how mastering the Five Strategies for A Success Life can empower you in both your personal and professional career?

Do you want to say "NO TO THE PITY PARTY" and achieve the life you truly desire?

Vivian Stark is an inspirational speaker and corporate trainer living in Vancouver, B.C. Canada, whose captivating story will inspire you to live the life you want if you never, never, never give up on what's important – You.

As a generational and workplace effectiveness expert, Vivian's career centers around helping others work in a more collaborative and cohesive work environment. Her focus on engagement and accountability both in and outside of the workplace mirrors her personal belief of how you must take 100% responsibility in all areas of your life. Learn how giving up blaming, complaining and excuse making can lead you to live a life filled with peace, happiness and personal fulfillment.

To learn how you can incorporate her knowledge and expertise into your life and business with ease and confidence, reach out to Vivian at www.gen-connect.ca. Vivian is available for private or corporate speaking engagements.

Investment Success and Successful Beliefs

JASON G. CHAN

"Why are you chuckling to yourself?" my brother asked as we passed by an upscale restaurant one night. "Did I miss something?"

"No, not really," I replied. "Remember those two Ferraris that were waiting for valet parking back by the restaurant that almost everybody who passed by, including us, were looking at and admiring? I just realized that if I wanted to, I could buy both of those Ferraris with cash, one for you and one for me."

Of course, I never did that. But that moment stuck in my head because it was the first time I realized that, financially, I had done okay for myself. I made my first million dollars investing in the stock market when I was just shy of 30 years old. My second million came shortly after that. That's when I stopped counting. I stopped counting because I finally found some comfort in knowing that my family was doing okay and that I was doing okay.

A few years before that, my father had suddenly passed away. It happened in 2008 in the middle of one of the greatest recessions in history. My family was entrenched in debt and my parents hardly had any retirement savings, let alone other investments. My two younger brothers and I were burdened knee-deep in student loan debt. I was living in my parents' living room because the basement where I had been living got flooded and became too moldy to stay in.

For most of my adolescent and early adult life, our family cash flow was tight, and we couldn't even afford a decent study desk. I haven't done too shabby for a boy whose desk was actually nothing more than a door flipped sideways and propped up by four poles on each corner; definitely not too shabby as an investor for someone whose degree was in fine arts and graphic design. I don't have a degree in business, finance or economics. I don't believe we need fancy degrees or education to do well in finance and investments or in life. For those who likes degrees, later in life I was told that I actually got a PhD earlier in life, since I was Poor, Hungry and Driven. At the end of the day, it's not your degrees or titles that make you, it's really about your vision and your beliefs.

YOUR BELIEFS ARE IMPORTANT

Sometimes people ask me what I did or what I invested in, hoping to get some insight as to how they too can achieve what I have. They're usually asking about specific things I did, specific things I invested in, or tools I used. What they don't understand is that these things are not the important part. Belief is where it all starts. To achieve investment success by having the proper successful beliefs, mental concepts, and proper mindset is the key.

After all, we all act and behave in certain ways because of our beliefs. Some beliefs serve us, some limit or deter us, and some set us astray. They shape what we do and how we do it. Before anything even starts, our beliefs tell us what we can do because they shape what we think is possible and what is not. Therefore, having the proper beliefs, or shaping what you already have, is really important in life, and also in investments. My purpose and goal is to help you adopt proper, empowering beliefs and realign, even discard, the negative ones as they relate to investments. It is only with a proper mindset and a successful beliefs system that you can get ahead in finances and achieve sustainable, consistent and long term investment success.

The first and, perhaps, the most important belief I want to share with you is it's possible for you to achieve financial and investment success. Not only can you achieve it, but you can achieve it on your own by empowering yourself to take control of your finances and investments. If a poor boy who started off living in a basement with a door as a study desk, who studied fine arts and graphic design, and who had large student loans and family debt could do it, so could you.

"It's Possible" is one of my favorite phrases from Les Brown. He goes on to describe that one of the keys to changing our belief system and enabling us to act on our dreams is knowing that something is possible. To know that a goal or that dream or that something we want or achieve has already been done or achieved by someone else, is to know that something is possible and achievable. More importantly, that "It's Possible" for you to achieve it too!

UNDERSTANDING FINANCE AND INVESTMENTS IS A LIFE SKILL

One of the first questions people come across when it comes to their finances and investments is, "Should I manage them myself or should I get someone else in the financial industry, such as an investment firm or bank, to manage them for me?"

Not only am I an individual investor who manages my own finances, I have also worked in the financial services industry, for one of the largest financial institutions in the country, as an investment sales representative for over 10 years. I am also a certified life coach who specializes in finance and investments. Through my various experiences, my short answer is that you should eventually invest in yourself and invest for yourself. Being able to take control and take charge of your finances and investments is a very liberating feeling that everyone should enjoy.

The investment service industry has a purpose and a place in everybody's life, but by no means should it be used or regarded as a long-term solution. It's like riding a bicycle with training wheels. Many people dream of financial freedom, but they are often dependent on an investment company to get them there. How could you be free and dependent at the same time?

Understanding finance and investments is a necessity in life. Just like eating and cooking, it's something we have to do for the rest of our lives. For this reason, I believe it's a life skill we should all acquire and develop. We have to deal with money, so we need to understand finance. Unless we spend every dime we earn or put everything under a mattress, we all have to invest. At the end of the day, nobody cares more about your financial future and well-being more than you.

HAVING SOMEONE ELSE MANAGE YOUR MONEY IS MORE COSTLY THAN YOU THINK

When it comes to eating, we won't eat out every meal, every day for the rest of our lives. We won't do that because we know it doesn't make sense and it gets expensive. So why would it make sense to pay someone else or a company to manage your investments every day for the rest of your life? Well, many people actually do that. One of the main reasons is because the investment industry has presented their fees in a way that seems deceivingly small and inexpensive. That's why many people don't mind "dining out" their whole lives.

Let's use the mutual fund industry as an example. The mutual fund industry is what most people are exposed to and familiar with when it comes to professional investment management. Aside from possible front-load and back-load fees and commissions, all mutual funds charge what they call a management expense ratio or MER. The MER alone for the average mutual fund ranges from approximately 2% - 2.5% a year. We'll take the low end of 2% to give them the benefit of the doubt. A 2% annual fee sounds small and nominal, doesn't it? The financial industry usually does not take the time or effort to explain what this fee actually means. Often customers are left with the impression that they get charged 2% MER from the gains that the company makes for them, if any.

In reality, that 2% MER is calculated and charged based on the entire amount of money they are managing for the customer, or what they call assets under management. What that means is, if you give them $100 to invest, they will charge you 2% on that $100, so essentially $2. Say you have $100,000 invested with them. At 2% MER, that works out to be $2,000 a year. For those who wish to have $1,000,000 ($1 Million dollars) a 2% MER would cost them $20,000 a year! To look at it from another perspective, a 2% MER fee in 5 years alone, works out to 10% (2% x 5). In 10 years, that works out to be 20% (2% x 10). In a mere 5 years and 10 years respectively, you would have paid out 10% and 20% of your hard-earned money in MER fees. Now consider that most people save and invest for retirement for about 35 years, how does the math work out for a long duration like that?

As I mentioned, the financial and investment industry is a business. Just like the restaurant industry and eating out, there is a time and place for services like that. However, it should not be used as a long-term solution, because it becomes very costly in the long run. I feel a true investment company and professional should be promoting financial freedom and independence, not financial dependence. Understanding finance and investments is truly a life skill that we should all acquire and develop. We can't afford not to.

In the examples above, I purposely kept the math simple and to the point and avoided financial jargon, such as compounding, time value, etc., because those are the kind of things that deter from the basic idea and confuse clients. The investment industry will critique our example and try to say that they will grow the client's money through the years. However, at the end of day, they cannot guarantee you any gains. So we won't factor that in. And to be fair, I won't assume they'll lose your money either. I kept it neutral in my example— no gains, no losses—similar to the "lost decade" that we experienced in the stock markets not too long ago.

INVESTING IS LIKE TREASURE HUNTING

When most people think of the world of investments and finance it seems overwhelmingly complex. A simple and interesting analogy I use to compare the world of investing and the investment industry is a big treasure hunt. If we were to look at it from this perspective, we would get a better understanding of how things work, many things would become apparent and begin to make sense.

So off to treasure hunting we go. Imagine we are in a world where treasure hunting is a big deal and almost everybody is out to find some treasure. Opinions on how to find treasure are a dime a dozen and everybody has their ideas and opinions.

Yet, despite the abundance of ideas and strategies floating around, many of these ideas tend to be passed around by people who have never found any significant treasure themselves. They hear and get these ideas and concepts from family members, a friend, a friend of a friend, and various media outlets. And where did many of these ideas originate from? A lot of these ideas actually came about through the "treasure hunting industry."

Yes, treasure hunting is such a big deal, there's actually a treasure hunting industry which is supposedly there to help you and guide you to find treasure. There are big corporate institutions with many employees who sell you treasure maps, treasure guides, strategies, tools and gadgets along with various products and services which they claim will help you find treasure. Many of them offer packaged plans to help treasure hunt for you through their professional and experienced treasure hunters.

The deal is that you put up all the capital to be used for the treasure hunt, but they do not guarantee you any success. The only guarantee is that they will charge you a management fee whether or not they find you treasure. And if they do end up finding treasure, they actually take a bigger cut of your money. So you put up all the money and take all the risk and they take a risk free payment from you in order to help you treasure hunt. And there are no guarantees of success. It's a pretty good business model for them, but not such a good business idea for you.

At some point you might begin to wonder that if these companies and their staff are so good at treasure hunting, how come they just don't focus on that and treasure hunt for themselves? Eventually, you'll realize that these companies actually make money from selling treasure hunting packages and products and by providing treasure hunting services. They don't make their money from actually finding treasure, per se.

Their frontline staff, sales representatives and professional treasure hunters, can give you all sorts of treasure hunting advice, ideas, and strategies, along with various treasure products and services the company has to offer. However, like most regular people, most of them have never found success in treasure hunting. The majority of their income actually comes from working their sales jobs and earning commission selling treasure hunting packages, products and services.

Sometimes you see some of these sales people enjoying the luxuries of life which can create the impression that they have actually found treasure from treasure hunting, but the reality is, they were actually just a successful sales person, not a successful treasure hunter.

Remember how we said that much of the common investment advice that floats around in public originated from these treasure hunting companies in the treasure hunting industry? A lot of the time this supposed treasure hunting advice is actually based on half-truths that are either outdated, have lost effectiveness, or have never been useful at all. They are mainly ideas and strategies used to promote and sell various treasure hunting packages, products and services.

There are actually really good and skillful treasure hunters out there. As you would expect, most of them spend their time treasure hunting for themselves. Some do open up treasure hunting companies to help others find treasure, but they usually require clients with lots of money and many of them have reached capacity and have stopped taking on new clients.

Keep this treasure hunting analogy in mind the next time you think about investments and the investment industry. It should give you an idea of how to make sense of it all and help you decide if you really wish to have someone else treasure hunt for you or not.

THE INVESTMENT LANDSCAPE HAS CHANGED

Since the new millennium, the stock market and investment landscape has been a lot different than it was in previous decades. This is not just a belief—it is a fact. It is important that we recognize and acknowledge this reality and incorporate it into our belief system for two main reasons.

First of all, in order to invest successfully and navigate through the stock market, we need to understand what kind of landscape and environment we are currently in. Imagine you are taking a road trip, how could you expect a to get from point A to point B if you were using an old and dated road map from many decades ago? I am sure it would be a frustrating trip with a few wrong turns here and there.

Secondly, understanding how the stock market and investment landscape used to be can help us understand where many investment ideas and strategies we still hear and read about came to be. More important is why they have lost relevance, effectiveness and significance.

Using the beginning of the new millennium, the year 2000, as a benchmark for the midpoint year of reference, let us take a look at the last 36 years of the S&P500, a popular and widely followed North American stock index. We will take a look and compare the 18 years prior to the new millennium and 18 years since the new millennium. So from 1982 to 2000, compared to 2000 to 2018.

In terms of returns, if you were to just buy and hold from the beginning of 1982 to the beginning of 2000, the 18 years prior to 2000, the total return of the S&P 500 was approximately 1,100%. From the beginning of 2000 to the beginning of 2018, the last 18 years, the total return of the S&P 500 was approximately 92%. A 1,110% return compared to a 92% return. That's a difference of almost 12 times.

In terms of declines and recovery, between 1982 and 2000, the two biggest drops were Black Monday of 1987, which saw an approximately 36% drop from top to bottom, which took 8 months to break even, and August of 1998 which saw an approximately 23% drop from top to bottom, which took less than 2 months to break even.

In terms of declines and recovery, between 2000 and 2018, the two biggest drops were an approximately 50% drop during the years from early 2000 to early 2003. If you happened to have bought at the peak, it would have taken you about 7.5 years to break even. Then an approximately 57% drop from mid 2007 to early 2009. If you happened to have bought at the peak, it would have taken you about 6 years to break even.

From 1982 to 2000, there was a 23% to 36% drop, with a recovery time of 2 to 8 months, compared to the years from 2000 to 2018, in which there was a 50% to 57% drop, with a recovery time of 6 to 7.5 years. From declines to recoveries, there was a dramatic difference in magnitude.

To summarize, it is important that we recognize and acknowledge that the investment landscape has changed a lot in the last 20 years because many investment strategies and ideologies we still hear today were developed during that comparatively stable and less volatile time. However, due to the changes we have seen in the last 20 years, many of these strategies and ideologies have lost their effectiveness, value, and relevance. The conclusion is, since our investment landscape has changed and evolved, we too need to evolve and adapt our investment strategies to the present. We cannot just keep on blindly using what has worked in the past.

WE INVEST IN OUR BELIEFS, NOT THE MARKETS

As we started off by mentioning, beliefs are very important when it comes to investing. They affect how we invest: if we take charge of our investments ourselves, have someone else invest for us or if we even invest at all. More importantly, I have to stress the importance of adopting the right and proper beliefs because ultimately when we are investing, we are investing in our beliefs. People often think they are investing in the markets, but actually what they are investing in is their beliefs about the markets. This is a critical concept to keep in mind. Personally, understanding and realizing that concept helped take my investments to the next level.

This reality might be a little difficult to wrap our heads around at first, but consider this, the markets behave the same for everyone. If we are just investing in the markets, we should all get similar if not identical results. But we don't. How come some people make more money than others in a rising market, for example? Or how come some are able to profit from a recession while others lose a fortune? The market's behaviour and performance does not vary from one person to another. It is the beliefs about the markets that vary from one person to another. Therefore, one of the main keys to being able to invest successfully is to have the proper beliefs in regards to investing and the markets.

GENUINE INVESTMENT ADVICE AND POOR INVESTMENT ADVICE

Many of our beliefs regarding investments have been acquired and shaped by various pieces of investment advice we've come across over time. And there's all sorts of investment concepts, strategies, and theories. Which ones serves us? Which ones do not? There was a time when it was tough getting information, let alone getting information in a timely manner. But today, with the evolution of technology via computers, smartphones and the internet, we live in a time of information overload. Investment ideas and strategies are a dime a dozen. Almost everyone seems to have an idea of what to do. We come across so many investment ideas and so much advice. Often, the more we learn the more confused we get, as many of these investment ideas seem to contradict each other. How do we organize and conceptualize them all in a context that makes sense? As an individual investor I, too, had to struggle with that problem.

After years of study, research and practical hands-on experience investing my own money, as well as working in the finance and investment sales industry, I was finally able to sort and put everything in context. This belief system is a mental construct meant to organize all the ideas, advice, theories, strategies, and concepts I've accumulated as they relate to investments. I'll just refer to all of that as "investment advice" for simplicity.

It's obvious there's some investment advice that works and some that does not. So, I separate them into two categories: "Genuine Investment Advice" and "Poor Investment Advice." Within those two categories, there are actually two sub-categories we could further separate the investment advice into.

Within Genuine Investment Advice, the first subcategory is investment advice that I believe is almost universal and works for almost everyone. For example, diversification, cutting losses short, letting winners grow, and waiting for favourable risk to return opportunities before investing.

The second subcategory, as well as all the other categories we'll touch upon, is where things get interesting. It's where it causes lots of confusion among people's belief systems and is a source of frustration for many. Within this second sub-category of Genuine Investment Advice is the investment advice that is accurate and works but may not work for everyone, because it depends on their personality and their investment style. For example, many investment ideas, theories, and strategies seem like complete opposites when you compare them with one another: value investing versus momentum investing, swing trading versus momentum investing, fundamental analysis versus technical analysis, short-term trading versus long-term investing, buy low and sell high versus buy high and sell higher, and top down versus bottom up investment styles. All these investment ideas and strategies work, but success depends on how they match the individual investor's personality and how they are used alongside their investment style. In a nutshell, those are examples of Genuine Investment Advice.

On the other end of the spectrum from Genuine Investment Advice we have Poor Investment Advice. It's basically advice that is not effective or does not work. Within this main category, it also has two sub-categories.

In the first sub-category is investment advice that used to work but is outdated because of the change in the investment landscape that we touched upon earlier. It used to work and perhaps even used to deliver great results but has since greatly lost value and effectiveness. Yet, these investment ideas still get passed around by many people because they have failed to recognize that the investment landscape has dramatically changed and evolved in recent years.

Some examples are: index investing, buying and holding indiscriminately, dollar cost averaging, and investing on a consistent and regular schedule regardless of overall market conditions. It's easy to see where such investment ideas, strategies and advice come from once we understand how the investment landscape used to be and what had happened in the past. Like we've seen in our example, the stock market, namely the S&P500, went up approximately 1,100% from 1982 to the year 2000. Yet, in our recent investment landscape from 2000 to the beginning of 2018, the total return of the S&P500 was a mere 92%—a return that's dramatically less than 1/12th in the same 18-year time span. That is less than 10% of the 1,100% return the we've seen from 1982 to the year 2000.

The second subcategory of Poor Investment Advice is the one which I despise the most. They are essentially "investment advice" that was never effective and never worked. For example, advice such as "If you don't sell your losing position, you aren't really losing money because unless you cash out, it's only a paper loss." That is as foolish as saying "If you go to the casino and convert your cash into casino chips, then you lose your chips, you're not actually losing money unless you convert those chips back into cash." Then there's "Adding to losses and losing positions is beneficial because when you average down, it gives you better value and a lower overall price point." With this strategy, you are not only not cutting your losses, you are adding to an already losing position. Technically, you could use this flawed logic to invest in a company as it goes all the way down to bankruptcy because it suggests the lower the price goes, the more you should invest. There is also "Focus on the long-term, and don't worry that your stocks are down because you're still getting paid dividends." Focusing solely on dividends presents a very distorted and partial picture, as you should be focusing on total return which consists of dividends plus any capital gains or losses. With that in mind, if your stock is down -40%, it would be foolish to say it's alright because you're receiving a 3% dividend yield.

People often ask, "If such investment advice doesn't work, then why do people say these things?" The answer is because these ideas mainly originate and get spread around by unscrupulous individuals in the financial and investment industry. In reality, such investment advice was merely conjured up to promote and sell investment products to customers and keep their customers invested so they could continue to charge them various fees and commissions.

Unfortunately, because much of this investment advice came from individuals within the financial and investment industry, it gave them a false sense of credibility and such bad advice got perpetually circulated. This is especially true because the advice is usually mixed in with some rationalization and half truths. When I say half truths, I am also referring to the dated investment advice that we mentioned earlier. I consider those half truths, because those strategies used to work, but have greatly lost significance since. Nevertheless, such bad advice is still often used as sales pitches by individuals in the industry to promote and sell various investment products.

Notice that all such advice falls under a similar underlying idea. It is to tell the customer that it is always a good time to invest and once they are invested, to never sell. For example, when the markets are high, they will say you should invest more because things are going well and you are making money. When the markets are low, they will say you should invest more because you are getting good value. Also, it is always a good time to invest, regardless of how the overall market condition is, because it is supposedly about your time in the markets, not timing the markets. Basically, the message is always geared at giving them your money, keeping it with them and never taking it away, so they can continuously charge you various fees. At the end of the day, if the client makes money, all the better, but even if they don't, the individual and company still gets to charge their fees.

In providing Genuine Investment Advice verses Poor Investment Advice, an individual's salary and bonus often comes in between the two. I'm reminded of a quote from Upton Sinclair: "It is difficult to get a man to understand something, when his salary depends on his not understanding it." However, to be fair, many of those who work in the financial and investment industry are not unscrupulous or ill-intentioned. Like many everyday people, they too, are caught up in the confusion. They come across poor investment advice that they actually believe to be true, which they use themselves and also end up passing on.

ADDITIONAL INVESTMENT TIPS FOR THE EVERYDAY INVESTOR

Make Use of Technical Analysis

As individual investors, we have limited time and resources. I believe the most efficient and effective way for an individual investor to conduct market research and to look for investment opportunities is through the use of technical analysis. Before you get intimidated, technical analysis is basically a fancy way of saying to look at price charts and graphs. You are literally looking at a picture, the big picture. It's efficient because, for example, if I wanted to, I could literally look through hundreds of companies and their price charts in a day. Comparatively, I cannot read through hundreds of annual reports or articles a day.

Keep an Investing Journal

Experiencing losses due to bad judgements or mistakes is part of every investor's journey. Unfortunately, when it comes to investing, making mistakes usually translates to losing money. At least when losses and mistakes occur, try to profit from them by keeping a journal of what happened and how, in an effort to learn from the experience and to not to let it happen again. As the saying goes, "Fool me once, shame on you. Fool me twice, shame on me."

Be Sure to Diversify

Diversification is a simple risk management technique we should all make use of to protect ourselves from the unknown and to improve our risk to return ratio. The simple reason being we can never foresee and predict everything in the markets. During my years of investing, I've seen an oil company whose oil rig was destroyed by a natural disaster; a factory that, due to some employee's negligence, was burned down to a crisp; the CEO of a company who got caught up in various alleged scandals leading to the collapse of the company and, one of my favorites, which is when Tesla's stock price took a sudden dive one day because Elon Musk decided to announce that the company was going bankrupt as an April Fool's Day joke in 2018. No matter how much in-depth research we conduct, nobody could have foreseen any of those events happening. So protect your investment portfolio by diversifying.

Look Beyond "Glam Stocks"

When individuals share their investment holdings with me, I often notice that they have many of the same stock holdings. The reason is they often have what I call "Glam Stocks." These are the glamorous stocks we often hear about in the news and media, the ones our friends and family talk about at dinner parties and gatherings. There is nothing wrong with having those holdings per se, but expand your scope, look further and dig deeper. You will realize that there are plenty of more diverse opportunities out there, many of which are either less volatile and less risky, have more growth potential, have a better performance record or sometimes all of the above. So keep looking and don't settle just for what you hear or see around you.

Know When to Get Out, Before You Get In

Before you get into an investment position, decide when you would exit if things do not go as intended. You are more clear minded before you start an investment. So decide when you would exit if things do not go your way ahead of time, as you will lose objectivity afterwards.

Gradually Ease In and Out of Investments

When investing, especially in stocks, a common practice is to use one entry and one exit into an investment position. Instead of using an all-in or all-out approach, a more strategic risk management approach would be to gradually ease yourself in and out of an investment depending on its subsequent performance. For example, instead of investing $5,000 all at once, consider investing initially only $2,500, then decide if you still want to invest the remaining $2,500 depending on the subsequent performance of the particular investment. Doing this would automatically cut your initial risk by 50%. The same idea applies to getting out of an investment.

Cut Losses and Keep Them Small

When investing, keeping control of our losses is a vital component of risk management. If there is one common piece of advice I've gathered from many great investors, it is that they all cut their losses and keep them small. Considering that most big losses usually started off as small losses, there is no point in letting a small loss grow into a big loss. If you are uncertain about an investment holding, instead of holding all of it or none of it, consider selling a portion of it. For example, if you sell half of it, you will reduce your risk by 50%. Another common culprit that leads investors to hold onto losses is focusing on break-even points and prices. In reality, nobody actually cares where or at what price you bought an investment and where you would break-even. It has no special meaning to anybody other than you and the tax department, so do not focus on that.

Avoid Adding to Losing Positions

When you have a losing investment position, often people believe that buying more will get you better value as you average down your overall price point. That is actually a poor strategy because having a losing position usually means that something you anticipated did not materialize and instead the opposite outcome occurred. There must have been something that was misjudged, overlooked, or unforeseen. Therefore, it does not make strategic sense to add more to an investment which you have already misunderstood and misjudged. Moreover, not only does that go against the concept of keeping your losses small, it is in fact the opposite, because you are adding more money to a losing position.

Remember that You Are Investing in Your Beliefs, Not the Markets

If there is one piece of advice that is more important than controlling your losses, it would definitely be that nobody cares more about your financial well-being than you. So understanding finance and investments is a life skill you should not only acquire but develop, and it all starts with your beliefs. At the core of it all, it is about working on developing your investment belief system.

This requires realigning and readjusting your beliefs and perhaps adopting new ones that serve you, while discarding those that do not. Remember that at the end of the day, we are all just investing in our beliefs.

FINAL THOUGHTS

Finance and investments are one of my greatest passions. I hope I was able to share some fresh perspectives and unique insights on subjects that I personally find to be rarely touched upon or discussed. The ideas and concepts are not exhaustive or complete, however, these are the big ideas, essential concepts and quintessential core beliefs that I've acquired through the years and which really helped propel my investment understanding and financial success.

Often there is nothing worse than to listen to someone advising you on how to reach your goals, when they have not actually reached it themselves. If there was a way for me to turn back time and have the opportunity to sit down with some successful investors who were willing to give me a few important pointers about finance and investing over a cup of coffee or a meal, I hope they would have shared with me the same pointers and beliefs I have shared with you in the last few pages. I know the insights would have definitely made my investment and financial experience a lot smoother and would have helped me reach my financial goals a lot sooner. These beliefs I'm talking about have helped me through many hurdles, make many investment breakthroughs and achieve financial success. I hope they will do the same for you. Remember, "It's Possible!"

For more investment insight, techniques and strategies, visit:
InvestingItWisely.com

Inspiring Leaders to Make a Difference

DR. WENDY SNEDDON

I wanted to change the *world*.
When I was young, I wanted to change the *world*,
I found it was difficult to change the *world*, so I tried to change my *community*.
When I found, I couldn't change my community; I began to focus on my *business*.
Now I realise the only thing I can change is *myself*,
Suddenly I realise that if I change *myself*,
I could have an impact on my *business*.
My *business* and I could make an impact on my *community*,
Then my *community* and I will indeed change the *world*.

Wendy's Version. Original Written
by an unknown Monk around 1100 A.D.

Have you ever worked for a great leader who is both encouraging and challenges you both at the same time? In 2012, I found myself in that situation. One year into this job and it was time for my first appraisal. Like most people, I was very nervous because you never know it was are going to go, but my employer quickly put me at ease, and it was a productive time.

Towards the end, he said to me, "I don't know how you are going to do it, but I want to be in The Sunday Times top 100 best small businesses to work for." This is a published list that UK companies can get onto and it is managed by The Sunday Times. I eagerly took on the challenge, but when I did my research and found out what it was going to take, well let's just say that I had serious doubts about the feasibility of it.

Much of it had to do with how our employees saw our company and most of them were not happy working for us. We had a fractured company based over 14 sites, and their only support was through me. How could we ever get the 3 Star "Extraordinary" rating required to be even considered for the list?

This wasn't a matter of changing a few known things. I had to start from scratch and figure out why they were unhappy and then come up with a solution that would not only solve the problem, but do it in such a way that our employees would tell others that we were the best to work for. There were times it felt like an impossible task.

BUT...

If there is one thing I have learned over my years of experience, it's that if you are willing to tackle a project head on and believe in your employees, anything is possible. So, I started by figuring out where the problem was and for that I designed a Happiness Survey. From that survey, I learned two things:

1. Most of the employees were not happy with their managers and how they were treated.

2. Communication across the entire company was poor. People felt disconnected and unappreciated for their hard work.

Now that I knew the problems, I could come up with solutions to help position us to be on that coveted list. Over the next six months, I implemented activities that would improve both areas.

I started with a weekly newsletter called Briefly Connected. We collected news from around the practices – I got people to send me interesting stories, shared people's birthdays and anniversaries and highlighted different people in this weekly e-bulletin and that became quite popular.

To connect people even more, I organised a company-wide conference where all employees came together for an entire weekend, where they received training and a special Awards Dinner which had a focus on recognition.

As I looked at the managers, I realised that this was an important area that would need a lot of focus. They were all excellent at their job but required training in management. As a result of this, I designed a leadership program for each manager in the practice as we recognised that people were unhappy with their managers and the way they were managed. Every two months we got the managers together, performed leadership and management training with them and gave them support so that they knew what to do when they went back to their teams.

Guess what?

When I had the employees do another Happiness Survey six months later, the results had greatly improved. So much so I felt we were in a position where we could actually move forward and go for the top 100 list and that year we made #48 and have been on that list, every year since.

A GREAT LEADER MAKES ALL THE DIFFERENCE

While there are many contributing factors to a successful company, one of the main ones is the excellence of the leader, because they set the pace for everything that happens.

How can you recognise a great leader? A great leader is someone who shares responsibility for running the business with the team. They give regular feedback on all aspects of the business. They look for areas where they can support, develop and do further training on areas that are needed, while always encouraging their team to go the extra mile.

They care about their employees and their lives. One leader I know, knew all of his employee's names, their partners' and kid's names as well. He remembered little things about them, so when he went in to visit people, he would ask them about their family life, everyone felt like they really knew him. People appreciated that he took the time to remember things about them and the initiatives he put in place, so in turn worked harder to make the company great.

TODAY'S LEADERS

The majority of leaders these days can be selfish and focus on their own position in the business and where they are going and expect everyone to do what they need them to do. I have known leaders who expect everyone to work their socks off, so they can reap the rewards.

A friend of mine had an experience where her boss had to reach a certain sales goal by the end of the year and promised that if it was reached there would be a specific reward given. My friend and the other employee worked day and night to reach that goal, and in the final few hours of the year, they did it. They were so happy and eagerly awaited their reward, but it never came. The boss got his reward and recognition, but this was never reciprocated.

After that experience, she felt demotivated, and the next time the employer promised a reward neither my friend nor the other employee even tried to work for it because they knew it was a lie.

Leaders need to keep their word and show that they are investing back into the company to reward the people, which in turn motivates employees to do more.

Many company owners are great technicians. They understand what they do, what they make or what they build, but they lack other skills (such as people, marketing or financial skills) and often don't recognize it. They try to do everything themselves and they don't know how to do many of the tasks well. They are afraid to admit that they don't know everything and they are often afraid to trust someone else to do this. They think that they are the only ones who can do it right. They have problems with delegation, and they don't want to let go of that control.

When employees are not trusted, or allowed to think freely and contribute to the business, they don't feel valued as a member of the team, and in return, they just come to work and go home again and are much less productive. They take more sick time and stress leave. They tend to be negative and drag other people down. This causes a high transfer rate of employees in and out, which is a huge cost to the business. All these things affect the overall profit and the viability of the business.

20 THINGS GREAT LEADERS ENSURE

If you check out some of the best small to medium size businesses today, you will see that they are run by leaders who all exhibit similar qualities and consistently ensure that all of the company's needs, including those of the employees, are met. Let's look at twenty of the most common qualities of leaders:

1. Vision

Great leaders have a clear vision of where they want the company to go and what they want the business to achieve. Along with that is the ability to communicate their vision to everyone in the company, so they understand how their roles in the business contribute to the overall success.

2. Passion

It is important to be passionate about your business. To love what you do as a leader and to inspire everyone around you to feel passionate about it too.

3. Transparency and Integrity

If you say you are going to do something, then you do it, no matter what. If you lose integrity with your employees, you will find that they will no longer go out of their way for you. Transparency about the performance of the company is also an important element.

4. Listener

Great leaders are good listeners and will act on what they hear. They need to be willing to do things like surveys and then be prepared to make changes. They can accept negative comments, learn some things about themselves and then change some things about the way that they behave.

Good listening skills include being aware of what is going on in the team, which means getting to know what is going on for people at work and outside of work, so when things aren't going so well you can spot it. This means when poor performance is going on you can pick up on it quickly and do something about it.

5. Communicate

You need to have systems for communication in place. How does information such as policies, training, and recognition get conveyed in a way that everyone who needs to hear it, does so? This is important for the productivity of the company, whether that's setting up a Facebook group, using a LinkedIn group or having an internal newsletter. It is important to find a way that works for everybody, to make sure that they all get the same messages.

6. Believe That People Behave with Positive Intentions

A good leader believes that the people in their team do things with positive intentions. This cancels out a blame culture where it is everyone else's fault when something goes wrong. Belief is powerful in that people will live up to what you believe in them. If you believe them to be good, hardworking employees, who occasionally make fixable mistakes they work towards that. If you believe the opposite, then they live to that too.

[1]http://www.cru.org/train-and-grow/devotional-life/personal-guide-to-fasting.2.html

If you create an environment where you work with your employees to fix mistakes, without playing the blame game, you will find your employees are more willing to come to you with problems instead of hiding them, and the problems can then be resolved more quickly instead of being left.

7. Responsibility

Give people responsibility, then empower them to do their job and to let them get on with it. Give them a clear brief of what outcome you want to see. Let the person go away and do the job in the way that they want to do it and as long as the outcome is what is expected, how the job is performed shouldn't really matter. This gives employees the freedom to develop things in their own way.

8. Reward and Recognise

A good leader should have a system of rewards and recognition. These can be quite difficult to implement because employers and managers tend to have their favourites. Therefore, any system has to be transparent, easy to understand, and be able to achieve that reward and recognition.

One place I worked at had a great reward system where we gave out everyone 'Alfies.' These were like pound notes, with a picture of Alfie, the owner's dog on the front, and on the back of it, you wrote who you were giving it to and what they had done to help you and inspire you. You signed your name and gave it to someone to say thank you. At the end of the year, you could cash them in for money or vouchers or gifts.

The emphasis was on looking out for the good things that people had done and then telling them about it by saying, "Thank you". This helped to improve the culture because people were looking for the positive qualities in others.

9. Fair Compensation

Properly compensating your employees for the work they do should never be considered a cost but instead an investment with a great return on investment. If you want to build an amazing team of loyal, hard working people who want to make your company succeed, then be generous with wages and the benefits that you offer.

10. Deal with Conflicts

How do good leaders resolve conflict? They deal with them quickly. They don't let things fester, and as a result they will go in and sort things out at the earliest opportunity. They also create a culture where people feel comfortable to come forward and talk about any issues.

11. Open to New Ideas

A great leader is open to employees coming forward with ideas and then taking some of those ideas and letting it be part of the vision of the company. Letting the employee work on the project where appropriate can also prove to be a powerful motivational tool

12. Be Yourself

Authenticity. You don't have to be perfect. Admitting concerns and flaws and getting help from the team is a sign of strength, not weakness. Encourage your team to come up with solutions to problems.

13. Flexible

Be open minded and flexible. You should have a 5-year plan, but you also need to be able to adapt this if the financial climate changes (such as the uncertainties around Brexit). You also have to be open to adapting to technology that comes along.

14. Positivity

Create a culture of optimism by encouraging people to make the impossible possible. You set the tone for your company and its employees, so make it a good one.

15. Commitment

When your employees know that you are committed to the success of the company and them personally, they will become committed to the company as well.

16. Training

Invest in training. First for yourself. Learn the practical elements of leading a team, but there is also that personal element where leaders need to learn to recognize their own behaviours: they way they communicate, their preferences and they really have to work on themselves first. Once you have changed yourself, you can develop a culture of personal growth and learning with your employees.

17. Being Honest About the Financial Data

Share the figures with your team. Get people to understand what the top line is, what the bottom line needs to be and what activities are going to help the company to get there. Help them understand where every penny in the pound goes and that sometimes at the end there is not much left over. They need to know how to control costs and maximise fails so that there is money to send people for training and to do rewards.

18. Understand Work/Life Balance

Do not expect people to work day and night and put systems in place so that they don't have to. Respect people's personal time and ensure they get it. Do not expect people to work extremely long hours, be on call and then work the next day. If it is required then ensure they are thanked and adequately compensated.

19. Well Being

Have a well-being policy. Set up a committee to look at all aspects of this and what is needed and what is not. Have a stress policy, carry out a survey to assess how your team manages stress. How can you help your employees feel better about work and create a healthy environment for them to work in?

20. Dedication

Your dedication is what is going to make the company work. If the boss doesn't care, then others won't either. The tone must be set from the top and then allowed to flow down through the company.

THE BEST STARTING PLACE

What a list! It may feel like a lot to live up to; the great thing is that you don't have to implement this all at once. It can take place over time. One of the best places to start is being clear about the vision of your business.

When it is just you, it is easy to have a vision and work within it, but when you start to bring in other people, it becomes more complicated. Having a clear goal of where you want to go with your company is a good place to start and explaining this to your new team helps them to understand what you want to achieve. Next, consider what you want the team culture to look like and how you want them to behave. The best time to design your ideal culture is before you have a team, but it is never too late to start.

One thing I strongly encourage you to do is to get the training and support you need to be a great leader. Very few people can successfully do it on their own and you are setting yourself up for failure if you think you can.

But what support is out there for leaders like you? Many training courses are designed for large companies with huge budgets and massive HR Departments to implement the ideas shared. What about small to medium sized businesses? Shouldn't they be able to benefit from training designed to help them and their employees?

Wouldn't it be great to work with someone who understands where you are as an employer and help YOU come with a custom plan that:

1. Helps you to identify the problems.

2. Looks at feasible solutions.

3. Creates a custom solution that fits your budget.

Well, you can. My company Lodestone Lounge was created for entrepreneurs by entrepreneurs. We specialise in helping you:

- With leadership coaching

- Attract & recruit the right people

- Provide the right environment for your team to develop

- Offer your team the rights and protections they're guaranteed by law

- Keep up to date with changes to legislation

- Have access to the latest and best HR advice through relevant websites and our in-house HR and legal team

- Provide your team with legal and relevant contracts of employment

- Write policies, procedures, and handbooks which work for your business and your team

- Have the HR software you need, tailored to your business, at your fingertips with our Great Employee Management System (GEMS).

Go to www.LodestoneLounge.com to find out how my company can help your company achieve its true potential.

The choice is yours.

Experience is Everything

Create Super Fans and Be Successful Forever

PURDEEP SANGHA

L iving in an increasingly competitive business world has made it harder and harder for startups and small businesses to become and remain successful. No matter the type of product or service, there is always the next great thing or a lower-priced competitor to entice your customers away. Statistics show that only half of new businesses last for at least five years, and a mere third make it to the ten-year mark. And, that's just the companies that get off the ground at all. According to Forbes magazine, about 90% of startups fail. If you're reading this chapter, you are likely a business owner looking to beat those odds. You may even spend a lot of sleepless nights wondering how you can keep your business thriving.

It's important to understand why so many businesses fail. Most often, it is because the owners focus on creating an amazing, cutting-edge product. That is a wonderful idea, that is until someone else comes up with a new cutting-edge feature or finds a way to sell the same product for less. Even if your business is booming, remember that companies fail in an instant, especially those whose owners and management have the mindset that "this will never happen to me or my business."

Instead, business owners need to focus on the one thing that has driven the extraordinary success of Apple, Netflix, and many other of today's most successful corporations: the customer experience. For years, customer experience has been a tool used by many organizations to enhance their business. It's become a discipline similar to marketing and sales. Customer experience is becoming more and more popular now as businesses realize that by delivering a high level of customer experience, they can easily differentiate themselves from their competition. And, when a company creates a product, delivery system or another benefit that enriches the customer's experience, that customer is much more willing to stick with that company for life.

People will pay more to be part of the right experience, even when they can get the same product or service somewhere else for much less. And, those customers are so loyal they wouldn't switch to another competitor even if they were paid to do so. They will also rave about a business on social media or to all their friends and family. Building a base of loyal customers can keep your business successful, and that means significantly less worry for you, the business owner.

Apple has actually created its own culture. Customers line up in front of stores hours in advance of the next iPhone launch to be the first ones with their hands on the product. This kind of devotion comes from more than just wanting a good product – lining up is part of the experience; Apple customers feel they are part of something special. For them, it doesn't get much more exciting than a new iPhone. They will ignore mistakes and faults in a new product so Apple's brand image is never really tarnished. They are Super Fans and they will even advocate for the company among total strangers.

Given how few companies have done a great job of building a substantial base of super-loyal customers, you might think that creating this kind of experience is incredibly difficult – like rocket science. I'm here to tell you that it isn't and that getting Super Fans for your business is easy once you know how. As a Business and Personal Success Coach, I have helped many clients grow to become extremely successful using this strategy. One of my clients currently has people eagerly waiting for his company to create a new product – they don't even care what the product is as long as it comes from his business.

So, how easy is it? Creating Super Fans is not difficult once you stop worrying about your physical product and start thinking about how you want your product to make people feel. It just takes focus, determination, and a little empathy.

CONTROL THE CUSTOMER EXPERIENCE

When you focus on how the consumer feels, you can start to build a strong emotional connection with your customers, and that's what turns them into Super Fans. As a business owner, you will want to control the relationship and the customer experience. To do this, you must lay out the details of how, where, why, when, and what you want your fans to experience. Creating a process for making amazing experiences is crucial, or else your customers could create their own experiences. Since companies are starting to learn the importance of this connection, you will need to develop this advantage over your competitors as quickly as you can.

When many of my clients come to me, they don't know where to start. I tell them to think about creating a connection between themselves and friends. Friends don't just have a single interaction with you. They have a series of interactions that come together to form their journey and connection with you. Acquaintances become friends, and friends become best friends after a series of positive interactions. The process is the same for turning customers into Super Fans. Everyone has a story of their own, and if you, as a business owner, can connect with your customer's story, you can create an emotional bond and convert them into Super Fans.

Here is an example of understanding and controlling your customer's story that comes from my own experience. At one time, I worked in the financial services industry. Our organization offered various products, including mortgages, to our members. Many of our staff viewed the product we were selling at face value, as simply a mortgage, but I explained to them that we were really offering our customers so much more. Our organization was putting our members into homes. We were helping them create an environment in which to raise their families safely. We were offering them a feeling of peace, safety, excitement, and even lifelong memories. In other words, we were providing a wonderful life experience, not just a mortgage. Creating that emotional connection through our marketing and advertising materials is what drove them to do business with our firm instead of any one of the hundreds of other companies on the market that can offer mortgages.

FIND YOUR SUPER FAN'S STORY

Finding the one story that will generate an emotional response from your customers, especially your Super Fans, is important. You can learn a lot by listening to what they have to say. Sometimes, their story may be amazing, and sometimes it may be downright horrible. It is your job to find out what it is and uncover what you can do to make their story even better. For example, if you own a detailing shop or a car dealership and have a fan come in with their Bentley, uncover what the car means to them. It may be a safe vehicle to transport their family, or it may be a source of pride that represents their years of hard work. You will have a completely different conversation with a mother of three children driving a Bentley than you will with a single guy working on Wall Street.

People love talking about themselves, so having these kinds of conversations with fans is not difficult. Ask questions with a genuine interest and people will begin to divulge all kinds of information. Then you are able to cater your offerings based on what you know about your Super Fans and their story.

The key in talking with your Super Fans is to make them feel special. You want to treat all of your customers fairly and equally, but also give them a sense of uniqueness, so treat each of them as your one and only Super Fan. A fan does not care about you or the fact that you own a successful business; they care about themselves. It's human nature to care about yourself first. If you don't believe me, let's do an experiment. Pull up a picture on your phone of you with your family. Before you read any further, please do this. When you just looked at the picture, where did your eyes automatically go? I'm willing to bet that they went to you first. That is what every person does because it's built in us to focus on ourselves. Everyone wants to feel special and unique. You want to satisfy your Super Fans by making them feel like you are always choosing to focus on them first.

The Disney company is an expert at making customers feel special. They have a terminology they use when talking about interacting with their guests. Specifically, employees are either "onstage" or "off stage." When a staff member is interacting with a guest they are considered "onstage," and their role is to cater to that guest on an individual basis. Their single focus is to identify a guest's story and enhance it. There are even signs posted in the staff rooms to remind employees that when they leave the area, they are considered onstage. As a business owner, you need to have the same focus as an employee who is onstage.

THE PSS FORMULA

Making your Super Fans feel special is the driving idea behind the PSS success formula. I created this method after years of research and learning from many organizations, such at MIT and Stanford, and years of studying the best customer service organizations, such as Disney, Zappos, and Toyota. Not-so-good companies dabble in the components of this formula; good companies focus on components of this formula; the best companies integrate this formula into everything that they do; and the industry leader in almost every instance lives, eats and breathes this formula (there is no life for them without it). If you consistently follow this formula, you are guaranteed success.

Here it is:

PSS = People + Strategy + Systems

(Interestingly, my full name is Purdeep Singh Sangha, so my initials match those of the formula!)

Let's start with the strategy because it is what aligns the other two components of the formula with the desired outcome. When many people discuss strategy, they use lots of business jargon to sound intelligent and sophisticated. They want you to think that it is a complicated subject. However, creating Super

Fans is about keeping it simple, so here's the jargon-free explanation: a strategy is simply a map of the journey that you want to take your fans through. (Think of it as one of those treasure maps in the pirate movies you watched as a child.) The strategy outlines the journey from where the customer starts to the final destination, which is where they are converted into Super Fans. Like any good map, it includes some interesting events along the way, as well as some cool characters.

There is no one-size-fits-all method to creating a strategy. Each business has a unique way of getting their fans to the final destination. For example, Tim Hortons creates value by serving customers as fast as they possibly can, while Starbucks encourages their customers to stay in the store for a period of time and enjoy the atmosphere. Both companies have Super Fans, but the strategy for creating and keeping those fans is unique to each company.

The second part of this equation involves focusing on the "people" your Super Fans interact with throughout their experience with your business. Your staff and any third party involved in servicing your Super Fans fall within this category. People can even include animals! Some retail locations have animals because many people, including myself, would sometimes rather pet a dog than interact with the owner, manager or even sales staff. Also, think about mascots at a baseball game – people go crazy over having the opportunity to take a picture with the mascot. For them, interacting with an animal or mascot adds something valuable to the experience.

Systems, the third part of the equation, are the events and vehicles along the journey. The events include every interaction your client has along the way, from the first time they work with your business to the time they find the treasure at the end of the map. Your goal as a business owner is to make these events as easy and painless as possible. For example, in a car dealership, the business owner should make sure buying the car is completed in a single, simple, and pleasant visit. Someone trying to buy a car would not become a return customer if the original process were complex and time-consuming, or if they felt the salesperson was misleading them.

The locations that your customers visit along their journey are also part of the system. These include your offices, retails spaces, website, and social media pages.

THE SUPER STRATEGY

I have created a list of goals that all business owners should have in order to create Super Fans. These goals will help you create what I call the Super Strategy. Let me share with you the first seven of these goals.

Goal #1 is to dream big or go home. The top 1% of athletes, business professionals, and artists are the ones that get the most rewards, so aim to be at the top. If you don't, you will fall short and hit the bottom. If you're reading this, then you have every desire to get to the top. If your business is doing well, great. Dream even bigger and better. If your business is scraping along or just managing to hang on, it can seem difficult to create big goals, but doing it is crucial to turning your business around. See how far you have already come by looking back to before you even started your company. Remember when you had nothing but a dream to be the absolute best in your industry. It was that dream that motivated you to start your business and to get to where you are today. Remembering that dream and building on it will get you through the tough times and back on the track to success.

The only way to amass Super Fans is to absolutely knock the socks off of your customers. Provide a level of customer service that makes them so ecstatic they can't wait to do more business with you, and to tell everyone they know about their experience. Whether you are one person running your business, or you have a team of thousands, you can do this – believe in yourself! Put customers first, and you'll do big things.

Goal #2 is to remember the end goal! Just like anything else in life, if you don't know where you're going, it's going to be tough to get there. I've asked many executives the question, "What's your end goal?" throughout the years and their answers often make me laugh. They say things that are so convoluted that it's difficult to make any sense of what their goal actually is! Keep your goals simple so that everybody in your organization can understand them. The end goal of any business should be to create Super Fans. Having Super Fans means that you can wake up every morning seeing your customers rave about your product and services, knowing that they are completely loyal to your business. When you have Super Fans, you don't have to worry about how to replace lost customers (because you won't really have any) and you can focus on creating amazing experiences for others, which will bring you a huge amount of joy.

Goal #3 is to be genuine. In order to successfully get Super Fans, you must genuinely care about your customers and make them successful at what they want to accomplish (e.g., get sales, speak professionally or take beautiful pictures that capture their travel adventures), as well as connect with them emotionally. Focus on providing the best level of customer service and success will follow. If you are 100% genuine, people will see your vision and feel what you are trying to achieve. Then, they will be behind you and support you every step of the way.

Goal #4 is that you must invest in creating Super Fans. I have worked with clients whose main focus is to cut costs while making as many sales as possible. But, long-term success is not all about the sales. Making your customers happy will cost some money but, the more you invest in creating Super Fans, the more you will get back in return. Just like any relationship, you must first give before you receive.

Goal #5 is that experience trumps all! Many larger organizations argue that sales and marketing are more important to the success of an organization than maximizing the customer experience. They believe that spending more on branding or salesforce efforts will generate more sales than customer relationship building. I call that BS! How many times have you, as a consumer, been sold an item based on its marketing and then been disappointed by the product? How did this make you feel? Marketing can often set unrealistic expectations for a product, and leave a customer feeling disappointed. Disappointed customers do not feel compelled to become return customers or to refer their closest friends and family members.

Future Shop and Best Buy are prime examples of how sales strategies can hinder or help the customer experience. Both stores are known as big places to buy electronics. Future Shop pays its employees commission, so when you walk through the door, you are bombarded by aggressive salespeople. This causes customers to avoid shopping there again. Best Buy, on the other hand, pays its employees an hourly wage so they can focus on providing customers an enjoyable experience instead of trying to make a quick sale. My guess is that many of you have never even heard of Future Shop because so many of them are closing. Best Buy is still around.

Goal #6 is to focus on the 20%. There's a popular business principle that 80% of the efforts, time, or resources spent in a business lead to 20% of results. Vice versa, 20% of the efforts, time and resources lead to 80% of the outcomes. That's because businesses most often concentrate on the whole potential marketplace, rather than the frequent or repeat purchasers of their products. This principle holds true for getting Super Fans. Whatever your desired outcome is, whether it's profits, growth, market share, etc. you need to focus on the 20% of your customers that help you accomplish your goal. Trying to get 100% of your customers to the Super Fan level would be frustrating and impossible, and it would cause you to waste a lot of resources. Instead, focus on your best customers – the 20% that account for the 80% of the results you are looking for. Imagine what shifting 80% of unproductive resources to productive ones could do for your business. It would be a massive transformation. Corporations are hesitant to do this because of the enormous impact it would have on the people within the organization. High-paying positions might go away because large corporate hierarchies are often inefficient. Small businesses are much more likely to make these kinds of transformative moves.

A simple example of the 80/20 principle involves the gym. The three main exercises that give you 80% of the results are bench presses, squats, and deadlifts. Most people spend about 20% of their time doing these exercises and the other 80% of their time doing exercises that are not that productive. I used to do the same thing when I was younger, even though I was a certified trainer. I spent a lot of time doing fancy exercises that I thought would get results but just weren't. When I shifted my focus to spending 50% of my time doing the three key exercises, I experienced dramatic outcomes. My workouts became simpler, I had a stronger focus, and I was able to measure my outcomes much easier. I reduced the complexity by 50% and increased my productivity by at least 50%.

You must be willing to give the 20% that represents your Super Fans' extra attention, to do things out of the norm, and maybe even bend the rules a little. For this 20%, you should be willing to do almost anything because they generate 80% of your results. They are the ones keeping your company profitable and letting you have peace of mind about your business. Remember that these are also the customers you can charge a premium for the amazing experiences you provide them.

The 20% is also the group that will give the best referrals and attract even more fans. The people being referred often have a profile similar to that of your Super Fans. As the old saying goes, "birds of a feather flock together." Those who were referred are probably already familiar with your products, the value, and the cost. Most of your selling has already been done by your Super Fans. What more could you ask for?!

For a small business owner, determining who the 20% are should not be too complicated. It should take a day or two to analyze sales, profits, and expenses to determine your Super Fans. If profit is your focus, your 20% most profit-driving customers would be your Super Fans. If stability is your focus, then determine who the most loyal fans are – those who have been with you the longest or repurchase more often.

Goal #7 is to give everyone a great experience. Focusing on the 20% is important to achieve 80% of the results, but keep in mind that even one person trashing your business can have a severe negative impact on your success. Thus, it is important that everyone has an awesome experience. Maybe you won't bend the rules as much or give them the little bit of extra attention, but you still need to make sure that every interaction with your business is pleasurable. So many organizations treat their top percentile as kings and queens and everyone else like peasants. Although common, this is a bad business practice that has consequences.

It is also important to remember that your normal fans can become Super Fans! As long as you treat them right and create an emotional attachment, they could easily become part of your top 20%!

IT'S EASIER THAN YOU THINK!

I know I said this before, but it is important and so bears repeating. Let me remind you of the first goal I mentioned, which was to dream big. Mark Zuckerberg and Elon Musk probably had no idea how successful their companies would become, but they did have a dream that drove them. Whatever your business goals are, I know that you can achieve them.

There is so much opportunity to create Super Fans and so many companies that still focus on sales instead of an experience. That leaves the door open for you to get ahead of your competition, especially if you act fast.

You don't have to spend hundreds of thousands of dollars to create a great experience for your customers. You also don't have to be a marketing genius or a fabulous salesperson. If you create an awesome experience for your fans, they will do all of the selling and marketing for you. Dedication, focus, politeness, and empathy go a long way in business.

There are many more goals and recommendations in the Super Strategy, and they are outlined in my book *Super Fans: How To Create Unwavering Customer Loyalty*. I also coach business owners, executives and managers. For more detailed information, please feel free to check out my book and subscribe to my newsletters at www.CreateSuperFans.com.

The Scary Truth About Lost Opportunity Cost

MITZY DADOUN, MASTER ASA, CPCA

If what you thought was true turned out not to be true, when would you want to know? My friend and business associate, Don Blanton from MoneyTrax, starts most of his seminars with this question. It really stops and makes you think.

We all go through life making decisions based on our value system of what's right and what's wrong. We assess situations and information based on the knowledge we've gained from the past—knowledge from family, school, friends, business associates, religion and our own experiences. We make our decisions based on this information.

Often the people we rely on for information are giving us the best information they can, but they may not have the background or the resources to really help us assess this particular situation. Our parents, for example, grew up in an era where people frequently worked for the same company their entire life, and they retired from that company with a pension. Our parents often lived in one house their entire adult life with one mortgage that they quickly worked to pay off. We live in very different times. People are much more mobile, and tend not to work for the same company for their entire career. Even if someone works for a company for a long time, can they actually retire and know that that company pension is secure? How can that pension be secure when so many "companies that will be around forever" are gone (Eaton's, Sears, Simpson's and Kodak to name a few)? Given the huge differences between our generation and the last, isn't it doubtful that our parents have the information we need to solve any number of challenges?

Technology is also rapidly changing our world. The jobs that were once stable are becoming obsolete and new jobs are being invented daily. What worked for our parents is often the exact opposite of what may work for us. We're in an ever-changing world—a world that's very different when compared to the world our parents grew up in, and it's a world much different than our kids will grow up in. What will work for us may not work for our children.

The reality is that often we don't have all of the necessary information when we're making our decisions. We're making them based on the facts we have at the time, not on the entire picture. The best example of this is the following simple ride on the subway.

It's a beautiful peaceful day. There are five or six other people sitting in the subway car. A gentleman gets onto the car with his five children and they are simply wild. He seems to be sitting there in a daze, not caring about the way his children are behaving. As the train is going from stop to stop, you can feel the tension of all the other people getting higher and higher. Finally, it gets to the point where I say something to the gentleman. "Excuse me sir, I hate to bother you but your kids seem to be going wild. Could you please speak to them and see if you can quiet them down?"

He kind of stops and shakes his head and comes out of his daze. Then he says, "Oh, I'm so sorry, their mother just died. We just left the hospital. I guess they just don't know what to do."

In that split second, I went from wanting to strangle the man to wanting to wrap my arms around him and comfort him in any way I could. In an instant I went from wanting to have those children be disciplined to feeling so sorry them.

(From Steven Covey's 7 Habits for Highly Effective People. It stays with me on a daily basis.)

Think about the following:

How did you feel when you heard about the rowdy kids? How did you feel about the father ignoring his wild children who were disturbing everyone? What thoughts came into your mind? And how did you feel after you found out why the man and his children were acting like this?

In a split second you had a paradigm shift, a complete and total change of how you felt and what you thought. The facts were always the same! You thought you had all the facts but you didn't. Please make the effort to keep this story in mind as you go through your day and as you encounter people. Maybe that rude cashier just received some horrible news. Be kind, you never know what's going on in someone else's world. A smile and a kind word can make all the difference in the world to someone going through a difficult time.

I'm very lucky I grew up in a safe and great city: Kingston, Ontario. Growing up, my grandmother and aunt always told me they believed in me, that I could do anything I set my mind to. I had an amazing teacher in grade seven, Sharon Bullock (Deline), who saw more in me than I saw in myself at the time. She really went the extra mile and helped me through a hard time in my life. I hope each of you is blessed enough to have at least one of those teachers in your life, a teacher who looks below the surface and really cares about and invests in their students.

I went away to a university that helped me start the process of expanding my mind, but I think my eyes really opened up to possibilities when I travelled and saw how different various parts of the world were. I visited historic sites and learned how advanced past civilizations were. How things like flushing toilets existed (albeit in a slightly different fashion), thousands of years ago. (I hated history in school but love it as an adult—I think the difference is my history teacher just stated the facts, but when you go somewhere, you bring it to life.)

I was lucky when I started my working career. I started working for a gentleman named Scott Cameron at Mutual Trust. He encouraged me to go to courses and expand my mind, to listen to and read Zig Ziglar, Jim Rohn, Napoleon Hill, Brian Tracy, Jay Abraham, Mark Victor Hansen, Robert Kyosoki, Raymond Aaron, Tony Robbins, John Maxwell and so many others. Over the years I listened to many great speakers who got me thinking and expanding my mind. They say most people read just one or two books after they finish school and hardly ever go to seminars. I've read thousands of books, listened to thousands of seminars and podcasts and attended hundreds of seminars in person. I'm something of an information junkie, as my husband says.

There's so much more out there than most of us realize. I encourage you to go to or listen to a seminar on a topic you haven't studied before. Expand your mind with new knowledge in new areas. If you haven't heard about or listened to Ted Talks I encourage you to do so. You can listen to talks on almost any topic and you can use the app to find any topic for any amount of time. You can listen to a 5-minute talk on astrophysics while you brush your teeth or a 20-minute talk on solutions to world hunger. Have fun, expand your mind.

ANOTHER PARADIGM SHIFT

The rich do things differently than the average person does. If we look at the population of the United States, over 70 percent of people earn under $75,000 a year. What this means is the wealth-building strategies you see on TV and hear on the radio are put out to the masses for those people who are earning under $75,000 a year.

The wealth-building strategies that people who are earning over $75,000 a year use are different from most other strategies. Robert Kiyosaki is famous for many books, the first being *Rich Dad, Poor Dad.* He goes through the different strategies that the rich use versus the masses. Napoleon Hill, in his book *Think and Grow Rich*, talks about the strategies for building long-term generational wealth. He talks about both mindset and the actions we take. Don Blanton is another brilliant mind, and his groundbreaking book *The Personal Economic Model* is an absolute must read for anyone. Don's book will help you see the strategies that are employed by the very wealthy, the strategies that everyone can use but historically only the wealthy have had access to and used. These are the models I use with my clients at Wealth Creation Concepts, employing uncommon strategies that help build long-term generational wealth, and create the financial security so many desire.

LOST OPPORTUNITY COST (LOC)

One of the biggest concepts that most people are unaware of is Lost Opportunity Cost, or LOC.

LOC can be explained by saying if you have a dollar, you have the ability to invest that dollar, and it has the ability to grow over time, but if you lose that dollar unknowingly and unnecessarily to taxes, interest on credit cards, etc., then not only do you lose that actual dollar but you lose the opportunity cost of what it could have grown into if you still had it. We all know we have to pay taxes, that's an opportunity cost we can't avoid, but we can work to minimize those taxes. We can work to ensure that we build our wealth as much as possible keeping that in mind.

You have two choices with every dollar you earn; you can spend it or you can save and invest it. If you earn 5 percent when you invest a dollar, your dollar will grow over time and become part of the engine that builds your wealth. If you spend the dollar, it will become part of someone else's engine.

A dollar is not just a dollar. It's also the interest you could have earned on that dollar as it grew over time. The LOC is what that dollar could have grown to.

Every dollar we earn has to go through a huge wealth sucking filter. First, the government filters off their tax. Second, we can spend and enjoy the remaining money, invest and save it for the future or do a combination thereof.

QUALIFIED SAVINGS PLANS

A qualified savings plan is known as an RSP or RIF in Canada and a 401k in the United States. Most people look at such plans and think, these are great! They think they can put money into the plan and the government won't charge them any taxes. What people forget is that they are just deferring the taxes, not eliminating them. They're sending that money to be assessed down the road.

When you put money into an RRSP, RIF or 401k, you're investing the money and any losses or gains that occur affect its value, but the taxes will be assessed only in the future.

If down the road you are in a lower tax bracket than when you put the money into the investment, you'll pay less in tax than if you had paid the tax right away. If, however, you're in a higher tax bracket, you'll pay more in tax. When you go to use the money in your retirement, or when you withdraw it for any reason, you'll be taxed based on the tax bracket you're in at the time you withdraw it. The tax man will come and he'll want the government's share of your money.

When you die and there's money in your qualified plan, you can usually roll it over to your spouse, tax deferred, but when it moves to the next generation it comes out as income and will often result in it being taxed at the highest rate possible.

Of course there are times when you can use the deferral to your benefit. Let's say you just got married and you're planning on having kids in five years and your spouse makes significantly more money than you do. The higher earner can put his or her money into a spousal RRSP. Then, the lower earner can withdraw the money based on their reduced tax rate at the proper time. Careful planning is required here because there are attribution rules. The spouse can't contribute to the spousal RRSP in the year you withdraw the money or the two preceding years. You can also put money into your own RRSP and withdraw the money during those years you know you will have little or no other income.

When you make contributions to a qualified plan you have to think about your current tax bracket and your likely future tax bracket. If you're in a higher tax bracket when you withdraw the money, you could actually end up paying a higher tax rate on that money than you would have if you had just paid the tax up front. Most people don't look at and think about the fact that the tax calculation is going to happen down the road. In effect you have set up a joint bank account with the government, you take all the risk and they tell you down the road how much of your money they want and how fast.

Think about it, right now the Canadian and the American governments have large, looming tax bills, are greatly in debt, have aging infrastructure, an aging population and they've convinced people to invest in tax deferred (which most people think are tax free) plans. Where will it be easiest to get money in the future? Where will it be easiest to increase taxes? The governments will simply increase the tax rates at the time when you go to withdraw that money.

WHAT THE RICH PEOPLE DO

People earning over $75,000 a year and certainly people in the top 5 percent of earnings and net worth do not rely solely on their RRSP's, RIFS and 401Ks, but rather on several strategies that, when combined, reduce tax, reduce LOC, preserve wealth and transfer their wealth to their children and to their favourite charities.

How many people think that with government debt levels where they are, government spending increasing, health care costs on the rise and the many natural disasters that have occurred and will occur, the governments will be lowering tax rates substantially over time for the "average" Canadian or American?

Tax free savings accounts in Canada and Roth 401k plans in the United States allow people to invest money with their after-tax dollars and have the growth on that money be tax free. I think it's an excellent program because you're paying the tax now, you know what it's going to be and it gives you the control on your investments.

LIQUIDITY USE AND CONTROL

When your money is in a tax-free savings account you can access it during an emergency. There are several other phenomenal financial tools where you can get multiple benefits from each dollar you invest. Knowing which tools to use when and how to combine them is key.

I think one of the things that people forget, especially in regard to qualified plans, is that you have a partner, the government. You have a partner that lets you take all of the losses, shares in all of the gains, and tells you how much of your money they want at a future date.

Let's say I offer to loan you $20,000. You are probably going to want to know what rate of interest I'm going to charge and how fast I want my principal back. What if I told you that "things are good right now, just take the money"? I'll let you know down the road what the interest rate is and how fast I want my money back. Would you take the $20,000 if you were obligated to pay back an unknown amount in the future? I might charge you a 20 percent interest rate or a 40 percent interest rate (tax bracket). That's exactly what happens with a qualified plan. The government loans you the tax money and reserves the right to change tax rates and withdrawal rates whenever and however they want.

YOU FINANCE EVERYTHING YOU BUY

You either pay interest on it or you give up the ability to earn interest on that money. If you pay cash for something, you lose the opportunity cost of what that money could have earned. If you finance it with a mortgage or a loan, you pay interest on the money, but you still have your money in your account earning interest.

One of the main reasons people like to pay cash for things is because they don't want to pay interest because in their minds they see it as losing money. The truth is you could actually be losing money if you pay cash because you lose the opportunity cost on that money and, depending on what the interest rate is and on what you finance, you could do better with your investments. I'll give you an example right now using a car.

Say you have the ability to finance a car. There are a lot of car companies that are currently offering 0 percent or 1.99 percent financing on cars. Now, say you have invested your money in a mutual fund, real estate or in your business and it will earn 6 to 8 percent. If you pay $50,000 for your car, you lose the ability to earn that 6-8 percent on your money. If you finance it you pay 0 percent interest, you spread out the payments over time and have the ability for your money to keep earning interest and growing. You also retain use and control of your money so if some kind of emergency occurs you can access the money. In this particular scenario it could very well make sense to finance the car using other people's money. If you're self-employed and can write off the loan, it makes even more sense. You're better off to take the loan from the car company! You get to keep, use and control your $50,000. You have flexibility if there's an emergency because you still have the cash available. You aren't giving up anything except for that monthly payment that you have to make. You'll also have the $50,000 in your bank account that you could use to pay off the loan if you wanted to.

YOUR MORTGAGE

One of the biggest assets most people have during their life is their home and one of the biggest expenses most people have is their mortgage. I want you to really stop and think about this. I'm going to share some very uncommon information, but it's probably one of the biggest areas where the rich do things very differently than most of people do.

THINK ABOUT THESE QUESTIONS

If you put down a large down payment on your home, will you save more than if you put a small down payment? If you have a 15-year amortization on your mortgage versus a 30-year amortization on your mortgage, will you save money? What about if you make lots of extra payments on your mortgage? If you answered yes to any of those questions you are about to have a paradigm shift.

I WANT YOU TO REALLY PAY ATTENTION TO THIS NEXT SECTION.

Let's say you buy a house (A) for $500,000 and you pay 100 percent cash for it, and I buy a house (B) for $500,00 and I finance it 100 percent. The houses are side-by-side and exactly the same. It's now five years down the road and houses in your area have gone up by 10 percent. The value of house A went up by 10 percent and the value of house B went up by 10 percent. Did it make a difference how much the down payment was or how much financing was needed to buy the house? No. The two houses went up by exactly the same amount. They are both now worth $550,000. They went up exactly the same whether the house was owned 100 percent outright or if it was 100 percent financed.

I'm not saying you can finance your house 100 percent and even if you could I'm not saying you should, but what I'm saying is this is one major area where the wealthy do something very different. The rich will finance the property 65 to 75 percent so that they will only be tying up about 25 to 35 percent of their own cash and then using that 65 -75 percent of other people's money and they will deploy and utilize that remaining amount in some other asset where it can also grow and create wealth.

So, if you take that $350,000 and you deploy it somewhere and you earn even 3 percent on your money, you now have your house which grew by 10 percent and you have another asset that grew by 3 percent. Or maybe you invested it in another property that you rent out and it will grow by 10 percent as well. Now you have two assets building your wealth. What about all the interest you have to pay on the mortgage? It's true you'll have to pay the interest on that mortgage but don't forget the lost opportunity cost comes into the equation as well. If you paid cash for the house you lose the opportunity cost of the cash you used to pay for the house. The house will go up in value the same amount whether it is paid for 100 percent or financed 100 percent. The increase in value on the real estate is not dependant on the down payment.

REAL ESTATE

Real estate has historically been one of the biggest areas where people have built great wealth. There are several great strategies to help you accumulate wealth with real estate. Real estate, when combined with the right type of permanent insurance, creates the ultimate combination for wealth creation and preservation.

INSURANCE

Insurance is another area where people often lose money unknowingly and unnecessarily. Some types of insurance are pure cost but necessary: car insurance, house insurance, term insurance, liability insurance, etc. Some types of insurance offer additional benefits and can be coordinated with other assets to shelter income, defer tax and even eliminate taxes. Knowing what type to use and when can make a significant difference in your wealth and financial security.

Building wealth requires:

1. spending less than you make

2. building an emergency fund

3. protecting your assets

4. paying down debt

5. utilizing strategies that help your dollars do more than one job at a time so that your investments grow as much as possible

6. minimizing taxes while accumulating wealth, when accessing the wealth in your retirement and upon your death

When you are looking at accumulating and preserving wealth you can think of it like a golf game. Would you rather have the skills of the best golfers or the clubs of the best golfers? Ideally you would have both!! The strategies I use with my clients are the skills, the various products are the clubs. Do you always use the driver or the putter? No. They do different things but are both extremely important. The driver represents the rate of return on your investments. It has the potential to go the furthest but is hard to control. The putter on the other hand does not hit the ball far but is easy to control and very often games are won or lost based on the puts made or lost. You can be winning the game for 18 holes and lose it all because of a bad put!! Properly structured permanent life insurance is the putter.

If you would like to learn more about these strategies, go to **www.WealthCreationConcepts.com** where you can request a phone or in person meeting. You can also call or text Mitzy at 416-993-2532.

Be the best you can be.

Ask yourself, "If what I think is true turns out not to be true, when would I want to know?"

Achieving a Better Legacy for Private Music Students

STEPHEN RICHES

Have you reached a point in your life where you would like to try a new activity or learn a new skill? Why haven't you? If you are like many people, a few failed attempts make you believe that you aren't talented enough to master the skill set, or perhaps you believe you are too old to start. The process gets abandoned and you chalk it up to something that "wasn't meant to be."

The reality is that this does not need to happen. Becoming talented is neither a mysterious nor a daunting process, but rather, like most things in life, simply one that requires a proven successful plan of action. So right now would be a great time for you to change your perception of your own ability.

In my first book, Talent CAN Be Taught: The Book on Creating Music Ability, I debunked the myth that music talent or skill is something that only a few of the elite may enjoy, and introduced the acronym, PRAISE™, which will provide you and students everywhere with an actual blueprint for successfully developing your music skills. Even better, many of these principles may be applied in other areas of your life.

Your ability to achieve can often be wrapped up in how you view yourself. Do you see your skills as the assets that they are, or do you find yourself setting up barriers to your own success? And, with the recent discoveries by neuroscientists that point to the fact that by developing music skills you also greatly improve your brain structure and function, there may be no better way to equip yourself for a lifetime than to invest in yourself with music training.

In this chapter, I will introduce to you the principles that I have used to help my students grow music talent. Some of these, undoubtedly, will seem very logical and straightforward to you. So, if you have ever dreamed of having music talent, don't allow your fears of what others might think to stand in your way. The first step, especially if you ever had lessons in the past but gave up on your dream, is to understand that the reason most students lose interest, become discouraged and quit is because the system failed to ensure that they received the basic training that they needed to succeed.

In fact, private music lessons have presented insurmountable challenges for almost all beginning students for many decades. The problems that arise are the result of the strategies used by most music teachers and teaching studios, rather than with the students themselves, who, unfortunately, are usually blamed for their own lack of success. And, the root cause of the entire problem is one that stems from a general misunderstanding about what talent really is and how talent is created in the first place. So that is where I start my chapter.

UNDERSTANDING TALENT

Many people consider talent to be something that is innate; something that you either have or do not have, and over which you have no control. This is, in large part, due to the ideas that most of us have regarding what talent really is. If we see someone who is very young who displays music ability, we tend to say that this person is very talented. But this begs the question that if someone who is older has developed the very same skills, why should this older person not be considered to be equally talented.

In other words, why should talent simply be considered the domain of those who learn more quickly or at a younger age? Should talent not be evaluated on the basis of skills that can be demonstrated, rather than the age or the speed at which they were acquired? Just as "the proof of the pudding is in the eating", so the evidence of the talent is in the performing, rather than the age of the performer. It is these special music skills or abilities that set talented people apart and which are an indicator of their talent.

A FAILING TRADITION

Whether or not talent can be acquired is something that has been debated for many years. But where there is certainly no doubt is that in the vast majority of cases, beginning students do not become talented. And it is perhaps this fact that has led so many people to assume that their failure to progress well in developing music skills was due to an innate lack of pre-existing talent in the first place. The truth, however, is that millions of people have been victims of a failing tradition in private music education. In my book, Talent CAN Be Taught™, I first identify the signs of this systemic failure, and then present strategies that are providing exciting solutions for my students. This chapter highlights a few of the main points.

The reality is that well over 90% of all students quit private music lessons within a couple of months to a few years and go through the rest of their lives unable to perform any of the pieces that they ever learned, believing that they were responsible for their own lack of success. The causes of this high failure rate rest with critical mistakes and teaching strategies made especially by parents and teachers.

I refer to one of the causes of this failing tradition as the Tom Sawyer School of Learning, after the character in the Mark Twain novel who is able to present documented evidence of achievement without actually ever having done the required work, or acquiring the knowledge that his evidence suggests he has. First of all, he devises a strategy to get paid by his friends so that they can have the privilege of doing the work of whitewashing his aunt's fence, which she had intended to be a punishment for him skipping school the day before. And then he buys Sunday school tickets from his friends the next day by selling their loot back to them in order to receive an honour which he has not earned, in the form of an award given to all those who manage to memorize two thousand Bible verses. In the end, however, the fraud is exposed in front of the entire community, as he is unable to even correctly identify the names of just two of Jesus' disciples.

It is an unfortunate fact, however, that parents, students, and teachers sometimes work together in a way that actually defeats the system, in the same manner as Mark Twain's fictional character does. Due to a quest by parents and students to achieve accreditation as quickly as possible, teachers fail to help students to acquire any of the actual music skills that are the real purpose of the lessons in the first place. Parents and students engage in as few lessons as possible. Teachers skip pages of the curriculum books, books of curriculum levels, entire levels of curricula, and in general then "hopscotch" their way through RCM grades to acquire a Grade 7 and/or Grade 8 RCM certificate for high school credits or to pad their resumes for future career opportunities. Some students have learned as few as a couple of dozen pieces over all of their years of private music training to accomplish this feat. They do not actually learn to read music, nor do they develop the ability to play by ear, which are the two most basic of all music skills. Due to the enormous struggle involved in learning advanced level pieces with undeveloped or under-developed reading skills, even students who manage to survive hate this process so much that they abandon the music they learned forever. As a result, there is a great multitude of students who have achieved Grade 8 level of Royal Conservatory of Music certificates who are unable to play even a single piece of music that they have ever learned.

So, to summarize the problem, some of the most obvious signs of this failing tradition are:

- Inability to remember and perform any music that was ever learned

- Inability to read music at sight beyond a very elementary level, sometimes even Pre-Grade 1

- Inability to learn or play new music by ear

- Deficiencies in technical skill development

- Lack of understanding of musical style

- A more than 90% dropout rate of all beginners every three years

Compounding the problem is that many private music teachers themselves have been the product of this failing tradition. In many cases, not only do they not perform publicly themselves, but they don't even perform for their students, despite the fact that this is the most effective of all teaching strategies. Further, despite their own weaknesses, they have no plans for their own personal professional development. And so, predictably, they continue to use the same failing strategies that led to their own weaknesses and duplicate these shortcomings in their own students.

The Powerful PRAISE Techniques™ explained in detail in my first book called Talent CAN Be Taught: The Book on Creating Music Ability are the key steps which form the blueprint for successfully creating music ability. The word PRAISE is an acronym for these six very important steps to success. Following is a brief synopsis of these key steps.

THE 6 POWERFUL PRAISE TECHNIQUES™

Performance & Repertory – The Core Essence of Music
Why the system begins with performance

Music begins with performance because music is a performance art. If music isn't performed by someone, it doesn't exist. A repertory is a personal collection of music that a particular performer can play at any time by memory.

Results & Accreditation – The Benchmarks of Achievement
The value of certificates and goal setting

While seeking to acquire certificates rather than usable music skills is to put the proverbial cart before the horse, accreditation does have a valuable role to play in measuring student progress. Awards and certificates honour achievement and provide goals for the achievement of excellence. These important measurable, attainable, and most importantly, dated goals for achievement are important steps in the learning process, without which all achievement is jeopardized.

Acceleration & Motivation – The MAGIC of Synergy™
The power of this element in the learning process

One of the reasons that so many students give up on themselves is that they perceive that the learning process is taking too long and they lose interest. Most students, due to poor strategies used by their parents and teachers, never are able to develop any synergy of learning. Acquiring momentum, enjoying accelerated learning, experiencing growth of skills and abilities, feeling inspired to become even better, and being motivated by competition, (either internal or external), to achieve as high a standard of excellence as possible, are all very important steps to success for everyone in all aspects of life. Becoming musically talented is no exception.

Insights & Strategies – The Philosophy of Education
"Only perfect practice makes perfect"

Talent CAN Be Taught presents a number of important insights and strategies for the successful development of music skills. For example, it is a common misconception that practice makes perfect. Student failures, in fact, are often blamed either on a lack of talent or a lack of practice, both of which fail to recognize the real cause of the failures. This famous and often mis-quoted Vince Lombardi gem is one example of a philosophy or insight that is presented in the book. What the legendary football coach actually said was that "perfect practice makes perfect". However, the reality is that beginners do not know how to practice, and bad practice never achieves good results. In fact, practicing independently usually leads to frustration for almost all beginners. All students need to be first taught how to practice rather than just what to practice. And students should only be asked to practice after they have been well-prepared for independent learning. This necessarily includes having some basic reading and ear training skills. Most beginners, however, are too young to understand and use sound pedagogical strategies for independent learning. As a result, independent practice often causes more harm than good in the beginning stages of training. In the early stages, practice needs to be monitored by an expert.

Supervision & Curriculum – The Tools of Training
The role of teachers and teaching materials

Private independent teachers, by definition, have no supervisory support. Nor do many follow a curriculum in its entirety to ensure that all concepts are taught. Many or most parents either do not understand or perhaps underestimate the value or importance of the role that supervision and curriculum have to play in a student's training even though it is taken for granted in public education. The music skills that we recognize as indicators of talent do not happen by accident or over time by independent practice alone. Like all skills in all vocations, they must be taught by an expert. An important part of the TCBT system is in making sure that our teachers are equipped to provide the most expert training possible for the students. This philosophy is at the core of all that has led to the great successes of our unique Talent CAN Be Taught™ system.

The most important factor in education for all teachers and students is the need for an outstanding comprehensive and sequential curriculum. Many curricula have weaknesses in the sequence or order that concepts are taught, the size of the challenges presented to the students, and in maintaining consistently small and attainable and progressive steps for learning. These shortcomings always contribute to frustration. However, the TCBT system follows what we consider to be the very best curriculum available, which we mandate to be used by all of our teachers and students. This is also discussed in some detail in the book.

Why is using a good curriculum so important? Well, first of all, teachers are able to follow it as a daybook to systematically track the lessons that they provide. And, students who follow it are able to avoid developing gaps in their music education that always cause the learning experience to become slower, more frustrating, and less enjoyable with every level of advancement. The irony is that the shortcuts that are often taken in the quest for faster advancement and achieving higher certificates at an earlier date actually slow down the learning process. By contrast, with the TCBT system, student skill development is occurring so rapidly that some of the students have progressed from Grade 1 to Grade 6 in only two years without skipping any grade levels or exams, and have achieved First Class Honours on their exams at every level while learning hundreds of pieces of music during that time.

Ear Training & Reading Skills – The Basic Fundamentals

"Do you play by ear, or do you read music?"

As a young person, I often had an opportunity to perform for recitals or other occasions or special events. Invariably, people would see me perform by memory and ask whether I read music or played by ear. My answer, of course, was "both". At the time, I had no idea how profound this response was. For what other method is there? Either you play by ear, or you read music, and ideally both, for these are the two fundamentally basic of all music skills. And yet, both of these important skills are among the common denominators that are missing for the vast majority of students who quit taking lessons after just a few months or years. They quit because they cannot read music, nor can they play by ear, and so they find it frustrating trying to learn mainly by rote and are not enjoying it. The Talent CAN Be Taught™ system ensures that ear and reading skills are actually taught, and these vital and basic fundamentals which are taught at every step of the way complete the six Powerful PRAISE Techniques™ that contribute to the great success of the students.

The Achievers Programs™

The success of the pilot program

The Achievers Programs™ were developed to ensure student success in keeping with the principles outlined in the six Powerful PRAISE Techniques™ that make up the core part of the TCBT system. The inspiration that led to the development of these accelerated learning programs resulted from the experience of one particular student and the strategy that I implemented as a pilot program for him. This student had chosen to begin taking a trial month of guitar lessons. He could not read music, and did not know how to practice, and had become frustrated very quickly trying to practice independently six days a week. Within two weeks, he had lost interest and stopped practicing. So we made a switch. Instead of guitar, we gave him a fresh start on piano. I made a deal with him that he didn't have to practice, in order to eliminate the tension at home that had occurred due to his Mom's insistence that he had to practice every day. We gave him three half-hour lessons per week instead of one, and I reduced the price per lesson as an incentive to invest more overall to the strategy. Of course, we also used the outstanding house piano/keyboard curriculum. There were, and still are today, five main goals of this program as follows:

- provide more frequent, regular, expert teacher support

- reduce per-lesson cost to encourage parents to make a larger short-term financial commitment

- enhance foundational learning with a switch to piano training

- eliminate the source of tension and liabilities associated with forced independent practice

- to create synergy among the various learning components with the frequency of instruction

Less than three months after starting this pilot program, I discovered that the student, who had been working with another teacher at my studio, was beginning the fifth level in the curriculum. And this curriculum had 4 books at each level. His mother had this explanation for how he had managed to go through 16 curriculum books in just 10 weeks:

"Oh, I forgot to tell you. He won't stop practicing. He practices at all hours during the day, even first thing in the morning before school. I put an alarm clock on the piano set for 8:15 AM. I tell him that when the alarm goes off, he has to stop playing the piano and go to school, or he is going to be late. I may be upstairs vacuuming and hear the alarm go off. I turn off the vacuum cleaner to listen, and the sounds from the piano keep on going. So I have to come downstairs to physically remove him from the piano bench and send him off to school."

So what happened here? Well, this student, who had previously very quickly become disinterested in the instrument of his choice (guitar), was now thriving on piano as a result of the implementation of the Powerful PRAISE Techniques™ that form the core principles of the TCBT system. I immediately began to promote these strategies for all of our students. Within three years, all of the students who participated in the program were able to accelerate through as many as eight levels of study achieving excellence at every level.

BUILDING A NEW LEGACY FOR THE FUTURE

An Innovative Teacher Apprentice Program

The best of systems can only reach its ultimate achievement when it is duplicated. That, of course is the principle behind the great successes of franchising. And just as many teachers are duplicating their own weaknesses in their students and thereby contributing to the continuation of the failing traditions, so the TCBT teacher apprentice program has been designed to continue and duplicate a new and better system of private music education. This program is designed especially for high school age students who have achieved RCM First Class Honours in Grade 5 Piano and Basic Theory. Students who have not yet achieved this standard of excellence, but who are currently studying at this level may also be admitted to the program. In the apprentice program, students are provided with an opportunity to first improve the quality of their own learning through examination of teaching practices and study of curriculum materials, to earn community service credits for high school by assisting beginning students, and eventually to earn part-time income through teaching beginning level students themselves. Those who progress to the highest levels of achievement will have an opportunity to become leaders of the Talent CAN Be Taught™ system to continue the legacy for future generations.

While piano/keyboard training is the best foundation for all music studies, the principles, of course, are transferable to other instruments and voice. At TCBT studios, we encourage many students to diversify and take a second instrument when they are ready for the additional experience. Some may receive this supplemental training in the public education system, but many do not. And all benefit greatly from receiving supplemental expert support with their band or orchestra instrument that isn't available in the context of a music classroom setting. Without exception, these students become the leaders in their school music programs.

AN AFTERWORD TO THE CHAPTER

In Talent CAN Be Taught; The Book on Creating Music Ability, I drew attention to the shortcuts that students were taking, and the resulting mine field that causes almost all private music students to get frustrated and give up on themselves within a few months to a few years. They incorrectly assumed, or in some cases were perhaps even told that the reason that they were not progressing was because they lacked talent, when, in fact, the real reason was due to historically ineffective teaching routines and strategies, and especially the ill-advised shortcuts that have been used by parents, teachers, and students for many years. These are explained in detail in the book, along with numerous recommended solutions.

In this single chapter, therefore, I have merely summarized and highlighted some of the key points of the book, while necessarily leaving out an explanation of most of the important details.

So while I hope that you found this chapter helpful as an introduction to the topic of how to ensure quality results with private music lessons, I encourage anyone who is serious about developing music skills to read the entire book.

In summary, the book includes a detailed explanation of many of the most common errors made by parents, students, and private teachers engaged in private music education. It also includes a diagnostic survey that will help readers to recognize if they have been a victim themselves of what I refer to as the failing traditions. Finally, it provides the proven blueprint for success through a detailed explanation of the role of The Powerful PRAISE Techniques™, as well as a number of helpful insights and strategies for success. These are critically important for all students of any age who would like to have great music skills, even for those who had previously given up on their own personal quest for talent, and who may now be inspired to renew their efforts buoyed by a better understanding of the proven keys to success.

TESTIMONIALS

"Stephen's vision and commitment to achieving a better future for private music education is truly inspiring. His passion for excellence, which I have been privileged to observe firsthand, is evident in his book's reflections and challenge for future engagement."

Reg Andrews
Administrator, Pickering Christian Academy, (Markham, ON)
www.pca.ca

"If your child is now or soon will be taking piano lessons, you need to read this book, because all students deserve to have teachers who really understand and value the important lessons this book contains."

Frank Feather
global business futurist, author, and father to two pianist daughters (Aurora, ON)
www.ffeather.com

"I took piano lessons for 9 years as a child and today, I cannot play anything! I thought that was because I was not naturally talented. If I had understood the concepts in this book – that talent can be taught – today I would be a professional piano player, entertaining people around the world!"

Dr. Robert A. Rohm Ph.D
speaker, author (Atlanta, GA)
www.personalityinsights.com

"I first met Stephen around the time he published his first book. I was so impressed with his commitment to making changes to improve how music is taught for the benefit of students everywhere that I invited him to be co-author of my second volume of *The Road to Success*"

Jack Canfield
entrepreneur, success coach, and co-author of the
Chicken Soup for the Soul books (Santa Barbara, CA)
www.jackcanfield.com

Declutter Your Mind For Success

ERIN MULDOON STETSON

"My baggage", "your baggage", "his baggage" —phrases thrown around in casual conversation as much as an actual suitcase is thrown around by handlers at an airport. What does it mean when we talk about our "baggage?" After all, we're not actually referring to that matching set of luggage your mother bought you after college, are we? No, we are talking about the emotional and life experience "stuff" you pick up along the way; the stuff that weighs you down and makes the inside of your head hurt.

When we take a trip, our baggage literally gets heavier and messier with each souvenir we add. And, if you're like me, you can't wait to unpack and put the dirty laundry in the wash where it belongs. Similarly, in life every experience comes with emotional as well as physical stuff. Unfortunately, not all of it is as pleasurable as the mementos from vacation. Plus, when unpacking, most of us take a look at what comes out of the suitcase so we can put it where it belongs.

But, when it comes to emotional baggage, people tend to stuff it away without really looking at it. What they are doing is filling up the emotional equivalent of a classic, overstuffed closet; the one where, when you open the door, a thousand things come crashing down on your head. The one where you don't open the door except maybe a couple inches now and then to stuff more things into the dark, scary closet.

On an emotional level, that stuffing is doing you no good at all. In fact, all that clutter is not relegated to your subconscious mind. It affects all parts of your mind, as well as your body and spirit. It causes pain, disease and emotional issues. It can block you in countless ways—from achieving your potential, living authentically and manifesting abundance in your life.

Why is your mind so cluttered in the first place? It's because you've been "collecting" experiences, memories and feelings for a lifetime. Even in the womb, there may have been alarming and confusing experiences. If you had a difficult birth, or traumatic first few moments of life, the imprint of those experiences is still with you. To add insult to injury, as a baby, you may have often struggled to be understood or to have your needs met while your bumbling care givers tried to figure out if you were hungry, sleepy or needed a diaper change. How frustrating that must have been. Those early experiences went into your collection.

Think about the clutter you have collected. I suggest that, as you read this, you jot down the thoughts that pop into your head. No doubt you will start to think of your own personal clutter that is stuffed inside you somewhere. Your notes will help you when you decide to clear that clutter out. Remember, you need to look at all of it squarely before you can put it away for good.

The collection of emotional clutter goes on throughout your life. In the toddler years, you stumble and fall (literally), and struggle to communicate only to be utterly misunderstood. Then, as a teen, you stumble figuratively as you try to find your way, and still find communication difficult as your values change in relation to those of parents, teachers or even your peers.

Think about it:

- A humiliating experience in class when a teacher scolded you in front of everyone.

- Someone you had a crush on treated you with contempt.

- A vicious, behind-the-back bullying campaign waged by an alleged "friend."

- A time when you were unkind or ungrateful to someone who didn't deserve it.

- The day you walked out of a store with a pack of gum you didn't pay for.

Each of these experiences is jarring. Every single one of them can disrupt the energy system in your body and mind. It's no wonder you feel so overwhelmed with the clutter.

I vividly remember something that happened when I was 12 years old. I received a scathing note from one of my "best friends" who happened to live across the street. It was poetic in its poignancy. "Erin, you think you're hot shit on a silver platter, but really you're just cold diarrhea on a paper plate!" Wow. That hurt. It's funny now —I mean really funny — and I'm so impressed with the verbiage. But at the time, I cried big tears —the kind of tears that I thought might never stop gushing. I had to re-think my whole persona. Did I really think that I was "hot shit?" And was I actually "just cold diarrhea?" I collected the anger, the sadness and the insecurity of that moment and buried it all in my mind, heart and body.

For the record, I'm not saying that any of the experiences I'm mentioning were bad, or good, for that matter. Nor am I saying that my friend in the "hot shit" story was wrong for writing that note. What I am saying is that our experiences stay with us, in one form or another, and often create disruptions in our energy systems.

Have you been able to jot down a few notes about memories of your own that may have stayed with you and created disruptions in your own life? Job struggles, relationship or parenting challenges, heartache, loss, trauma—the little things and the big things that may be stuffed away, buried, doing some damage unbeknownst to you.

All of these things go into your collection. Don't judge them. Don't judge yourself. Simply write down a "title" for the memory. We'll address it later and possibly let go of it with ease. You won't lose the memory, but merely the negative charge that is connected to it.

Now that you have started to examine your impressive collection, you can understand how it has grown exponentially over your lifetime. You can imagine how your mind has gotten cluttered. It's no wonder so many people feel weighed down, bottled up, distracted and even confused at times.

It is possible to declutter your mind if you have the proper tools. There is a process you can use to fix the effects of that build-up.

Pat yourself on the back for beginning this journey. It's going to be fun!

TAPPING

Tapping is based on Emotional Freedom Techniques (EFT). It is a relatively new discovery that has provided thousands with relief from pain, disease and emotional issues. It can alleviate the most common matters (fear of public speaking) to the most extreme (chronic debilitating back pain), and a wide array of "stuff" in between. Basically, tapping is mind/body healing. It is a combination of ancient Chinese knowledge and modern psychology.

Tapping produces a relaxation response in your body and mind and creates an emotional contentment in the present moment. It is wonderfully simple and effective, and it is accomplished by stimulating well established energy meridian points on your body.

"How do you do that?"

You do that by tapping on particular points with your fingertips while focusing on the issue at hand. "

Really?" "It's not more complicated than that?"

Yes, really. And no, it's not more complicated than that. Plus, the process is easy to memorize, and portable—you can do it anywhere. You only need your hands and your mind.

It is my goal to make this real healing easy and accessible to you. For the entrepreneur feeling overwhelmed, or the person who has dreams of starting a business but is blocked by fear, these techniques can help create such fundamental shifts that walls tumble and doors open. The healing path of body, mind and spirit lies ahead.

So how does tapping differ, say, from other energy healing modalities such as acupuncture? By focusing on the mind-body connection, EFT tapping harnesses the power of the mind and combines it with the body's energy to propel healing to a level that could not otherwise be achieved. The techniques essentially bring a psychotherapeutic element to the energy meridians long familiar to alternative healers.

The power of thought and its effects on our well-being are no longer considered theoretical. The evidence is piling up. So let's declutter your mind so that your thoughts no longer sabotage you but can have the impact you want them to!

EFT TAPPING IN ACTION

Let's look at a particular, very real scenario that will be familiar to many. I like to call it the fear of public writing. Now, we could also address the fear of public speaking or something else but, given the fact that I overcame my fear of public writing to write this chapter, it seems an apropos example. Additionally, the fear of public writing can be a huge deal for an entrepreneur, especially when you are expected to publish a blog, post on Facebook and update your website on a regular basis.

EFT tapping has the unique ability to handle your fears and turn them into calm cool action. Whether you feel paralyzed at the thought of doing an activity like writing, or are shy about sharing what you've already written, EFT tapping can help put those fears in check.

For example, have you hesitated to write a book because of your anxiety about the fact that the dreaded written word can never be erased? It will be "out there" speaking for you, for all time. If you are like I was, that thought paralyzes you. But here I am, writing this. And enjoying it, I might add. How am I able to face my fears so courageously?

As I mentioned above, the answer is quite simple and incredibly revolutionary. I can't wait to share this fabulous secret with you. Tap along with me. You won't be sorry. Then we can high five on the other side of this silly fear that's holding you back from your greatness.

EFT IN A NUTSHELL

The body contains a network of energy points and energy channels — actual locations that can be accessed through tapping. In addition to the physical act of tapping on these specific points, EFT involves the use of words. The power of words, of language, to channel and manifest intention is hardly in question any more. So with EFT, you will use words first to acknowledge the details of the negative — the big pieces of junk cluttering your mind.

Looking at them and facing them is the first step to releasing the junk you've been shoving into your suitcase for so long. Finally, positive language is used to manifest what you want to bring into your life after you've "put away" the clutter where it belongs. Where is that? It's where your clutter can no longer hurt you.

So, let's return to our hypothetical case of a person (maybe you) who is afraid to write. This fear is getting in the way of your business, your success and your ability to create abundance in your life. Below are the simple steps that I would walk you through if you were this hypothetical person. In no time, you would be writing and publishing.

STEP 1

Close your eyes and think about what is holding you back from writing and publishing that book or updating your blog. Once you have something specific in mind, give it a number on a scale of 0-10, ten being the most intense. If you have many things running through your mind, write them down and start with the one specific issue that has the highest intensity. Think of it as the biggest piece of junk in that closet—the one that might actually knock you out if it fell on your head. Give that piece of junk a "title"—you don't need to write down the whole sordid history or explanation of the issue, just its title. The number you assign to that issue is extremely important. It allows you to compare how you feel before and after tapping.

For example, you may be thinking: "What if my ex reads this and thinks, 'what the %&*# is she writing about? Why was I ever with that chick? What a weirdo!'" Or perhaps you are thinking, "No one who reads this will ever want to talk to me, meet me or hire me. I'll be ruined."

Your title for this piece of mental debris might be: Fear of Rejection. Maybe it earns a level of 8, 9 or even 10, depending on how paralyzing it is. (You insert whichever number makes sense for how you feel in the present moment.)

STEP 2

Tap continuously with your fingers on each of the following spots while repeating the corresponding phrases out loud. (If you think a diagram might be helpful, please visit http://taponit.com.)

- **Karate Chop Spot** (this is the place on the side of your hand you would use if you were to use a karate chop to break a piece of wood): Tap continuously with four fingers on that spot while saying the following phrase three times aloud: "Even though I am afraid of being judged and rejected [insert here: by my ex or by future clients] for what I write, I'm still a really good person."

- **Eyebrow point** (this is the beginning of your eyebrow closest to your nose): Tap continuously with two fingers at that spot and repeat the following phrase: "I'm afraid that my [ex or future client] is going to judge me and my writing in a negative way." Repeat Once.

- **Side of eye** (this is the bone bordering the outside corner of your eye): Tap continuously with two fingers on that spot and repeat the following phrase: "What if my [ex or future client] reads what I wrote and thinks I'm a terrible writer?" Repeat Once.

- **Under the eye** (about ½ inch below): Tap continuously with two fingers, saying: "I'm nervous to put myself out there. I will be laughed at." Repeat once.

- **Under the nose** (this is the philtrum: the small indentation between the bottom of your nose and the top of your upper lip): Tap continuously with two fingers on that spot while you say: "I'm afraid that someone [my ex or a judgmental future client] is going to read my writing if I put it out there." Repeat once.

- **Chin** (the spot midway between the bottom of your chin and your lower lip): Tap continuously with two fingers on that spot and say: "I'm not sure if I can handle the embarrassment of having my writing judged by [my ex, a future client] or anyone else for that matter." Repeat once.

- **Collarbone**: Tap continuously with four fingers along your collarbone towards your breast bone. Say these words: "I'm not ready to have my thoughts and ideas critiqued and ridiculed." Repeat once.

- **Under arm** (four inches below your armpit, on the side of your body): Tap continuously with four fingers: "I'm nervous that [my ex or a future client] will read what I'm writing and make fun of me." Repeat once.

- **Crown of head**: Tap continuously with all five fingers in a circular motion on the top of your head: "I'm afraid that [my ex or anyone] is going to read my writing and laugh at me." Repeat once.

- **Eyebrow point**: "I'm okay now." Repeat once.

- **Side of eye**: "I can relax now." Repeat once.

- **Under the eye**: "I am calm and relaxed." Repeat once.

- **Under the nose**: "My confidence is growing." Repeat once.

- **Chin**: "I am feeling more and more confident about my writing." Repeat once.

- **Collarbone**: "I am excited to write an awesome [book, article, blog]." Repeat once.

- **Under arm**: "I can't wait to write my [book, article, blog]." Repeat once.

- **Top of head**: "I'm ready to write and publish an amazing [book, article, blog]." Repeat once.

When you are done, take a deep breath and hold it. Then let it out in a slow, smooth exhalation.

STEP 3

After completing the tapping and repetitions, reassess the intensity of your feelings about the topic (in this case, public writing), using the scale you used originally, from 0 to 10, with ten being the strongest. Write down your response, the number and something about how you feel. Comment about whether there were any qualitative changes to the way you view or feel about the topic. If your number is still high, then repeat the process.

Be clear in acknowledging any change. For example, "After tapping, my fear of rejection and judgment regarding my writing from [my ex or future clients] is at about a level two, down significantly from my previous level of eight."

The three steps outlined above are how you use EFT to overcome your fear of public writing. You can use the same format to cope with other issues that are holding you back. The phrases that you use in your repetitions during tapping will vary according to what you are trying to release. Here are some examples:

- **Karate Chop Spot**: "Even though I'm afraid that my family will disown me because what I want to write about is too off the grid for them, I have confidence and love. I forgive them for their potential judgments." Repeat three times.

- **Karate Chop Spot**: "Even though I fear that my ideas will change one day, and what I write will be 'out there' forever, reminding me of how foolish I was, I deeply and completely love and accept myself."

- **Karate Chop Spot**: "Even though my writing isn't perfect, it's a work in progress that never seems to end. I am whole, and complete, and fabulous just as I am right now, and so is my writing."

- **Karate Chop Spot**: "Even though I feel as if I don't have time to write, I am willing to make changes in my life because I deeply and completely love and accept myself."

The intended and very real outcome of EFT tapping in this circumstance is increased self-confidence. Whether it is your writing or something else that is standing in your way, your confidence will grow exponentially the more you tap. You will laugh at your previous fears. To use our example of fearing the reaction of your ex, once you have utilized EFT tapping, you might assume that, should he read your writing, he'll wonder how he ever let someone like you get away!

Our fears about what might happen are often times more intense than any actual, potential outcome. Tapping creates equilibrium between that fear and what is real. It will allow you to gain a calm, cool perspective regarding the debris that was weighing you down by cluttering up your suitcase or your closet –in other words, your mind!

Decluttering your mind through EFT tapping applies to literally any aspect of your life. It can help you find fulfillment, success, and enjoyment in any arena: relationships, money, body image, health etc. Starting with identifying what is holding you back, seeing it for what it is and then releasing it, you ultimately replace it with something wholesome that will help you move forward.

The things that are holding you back are all that junk we talked about earlier: Fears or objections (the "I can't" mentality), obstacles — perceived or real (time, logistics) — and ultimately your "story" – the belief system that holds you where you are instead of helping you get to where you want to be.

The process that works for your mind can also be used to declutter your body. There is a holistic connection between and among mind, body and spirit, which means that detoxing one will help you declutter the others.

Your spirit can be decluttered and detoxified too. In using EFT techniques for the spirit, you will address matters of perspective, outlook and attitude. The law of attraction is essentially at work every time you succumb to fear or, conversely, feel optimistic. When you fear an outcome and fixate on that fear, you are focusing on what is essentially a belief system based on fear. Your mind, as well as your actions, reflects that belief system and you will manifest the very things you are afraid of.

When you can tap on and release the fear, you can recreate a belief system based on positive emotions, optimism and confidence. You become that person and your every action reflects those new beliefs.

So what does this mean for you? It means that EFT tapping can bring you more comfort, love and enjoyment in life. It can help you rid yourself of the heavy baggage and clutter that get in the way of being your most successful self.

To learn more about the benefits of tapping, please visit http://taponit.com.

How to Do I.O.A.L.

A Simple Financial Blueprint

BERNARD H. DALZIEL

T he tried and true principles of saving and spending less seem to be the only financial literacy that most of us are exposed to. For so many of us, that means we are armed with little knowledge about one of the most important aspects of our lives, which is how to manage the money that we all need to function and enjoy the experiences that give meaning and depth to our lives.

Throughout this chapter, I am going to share the I.O.A.L. system, one that focuses on four key areas that are critical to building your wealth and helping you grow your net worth. Along the way, I am going to help you gain a better understanding of how to meet your financial goals and positively impact your future. Let's get started!

THE BEGINNING OF MY FINANCIAL EDUCATION

I love to help others help themselves by providing solutions that can help them double their income and triple their time off. When I started out, it wasn't easy for me. I had a hard time growing up. I was definitely considered a problem child. In fact, I probably spent more time in the hallway than I did in the classroom!

Yet, that was not time that I wasted. Instead, I used it to dream and stretch my imagination, growing and developing my EQ versus my IQ. Since I was out there already, I got to know everyone. To me, a stranger was just a friend that I hadn't met yet.

I was ready to quit school at age 12. Yet, there were moments and individuals that helped me during this academic struggle. I had a counselor who taught me a secret that helped me to learn the 9 multiplication tables in seventh grade. At that point, I was skipping school on a regular basis. I was hauled back to school by a truant officer and assigned to a counselor named Tom. He became my friend, and told me that if I was determined to leave school, there were certain basic things that I needed to know, such as reading, writing, and arithmetic.

That was when he found out that I didn't even know my 9 multiplication tables. He helped me fill out a job application with a short quiz on it. One part of the quiz was the 9 multiplication tables. I had to write the multiplication table from 1 to 9, put four triangles in a square, and then mail it in. As I did the multiplication table, I counted down (see the diagram). Then I put an X in the box. Now I decided to mail it myself, but being dyslexic, I wrote my name and address on the front, and the address I wanted to send it to on the back. I forgot to put a stamp on it, but I did remember to put it in the mailbox. A week later, I received the call to come in for an interview for the position of an office boy. More about that later.

Notice all the things I did wrong, yet how it all came together. By putting the address in the wrong spot, but forgetting the stamp, the letter was essentially returned to the place that I wanted it to go all along.

I also read the book Psycho-Cybernetics by Maxwell Maltz. He was a plastic surgeon who found that individuals were no happier after plastic surgery, simply because they had changed their outside, but not their inside, which included how they thought about themselves.

I made the decision to change how I viewed myself. No longer was I going to see myself as an academic failure, but as someone with unique gifts and talents that I could share with others. I decided to dedicate my life to helping others to help themselves by providing easy to understand information. One area in particular that I knew I could help was by creating a simple formula that gives people a way to create a written financial plan or blueprint. It was meant to help them change the way they think about their finances and give them an easy step-by-step process for financial freedom and independence.

If the elevator for success no longer works for you, then I want you to have the ability to take the stairs, one step at a time. Most people don't plan to fail, they just fail to plan.

Granted, I still had obstacles and challenges to face. I was dyslexic, which made school a trial, as I mentioned earlier. Then I started down a self-destructive path, one that led to alcohol, smoking, and drugs. It was a way of life that could have cost me mine. Still determined to follow this path of self-destruction, I lost my father at the age of 15. Now, I had to stop doing drugs because I had to step up and help my mother. It was time for me to grow up.

My mother, Irene Richardson, is an impressive individual, one who raised her children with a sense of purpose and a desire to learn. Even to this day, she is active, and her routine could wear me out! She taught me that common sense is not that common these days. At the ripe age of 89 years old, she takes no pills, just nutritional supplements, and leads a water aerobics class 6 days a week. Her one day off is for God, and she knows that God answers all who take a knee.

As I got closer to 16, I realized that I needed to be a man. I stopped using drugs and got my driver's license. I also joined the swim team. I truly started to take control of my life and shape it to fit my vision, instead of allowing others' opinions of my capabilities define me. By 19, I had taken the exam for industrial first aid, and I became a first aid attendant and night watchman.

Then I took on an apprenticeship and became a distribution engineer in Vancouver. At that time, I was making $50,000 a year. It was a chance to party, and I did that until I was 37. That was when I met my mentor Raymond Aaron, through his Dr. Al Lowry course on investing in real estate. I also took a Thurston Wright course. My world was on a high. I cleaned myself up, mind, body, and soul. I took a year off to work on my personal relationship with my daughter. At the time, I was earning $5,000 a month.

That was when life threw up a huge obstacle. My marriage was ending. The divorce was difficult, draining me mentally, physically, emotionally, and especially financially. Suddenly a judge was telling me that half my monthly income ($2,500) needed to go to my soon-to-be ex-wife. I was in debt and going through the divorce from hell when I reconnected with Raymond Aaron.

I signed up for his monthly mentoring program using my credit card. I was adding more debt, but Raymond told me to give him two years and I would be able to change my life. I completed the mentoring program and I still have the certificate hanging on my wall. I completed my divorce and refinanced my debts to a comfortable level.

The next few years saw my life taking an amazing turn for the better. I met and married the love of my life and was able to help her raise her son and godson. Both of these young men went on to receive Master's degrees in their chosen fields. My daughter became an RN and now I am about to be a grandfather. My life is rich and full of blessings, but I realized that now was the best time to reach out to others and share a way to make a financial blueprint simple. My goal is to make complicated things simple, and help us all to achieve a life of peace in the process.

One of the things I credit with helping me to achieve this level of success in my life is that I took advantage of having mentors. Too often, we assume that our experiences make us the best guide to create the future we want. I learned that this is not the case. Robert Kiyosaki, author of *Rich Dad, Poor Dad*, also served as a mentor for me. His cash flow game, and explanation of how and why we work, helped me to make changes in my mindset. I also found mentors in Brian Tracy; Fred Synder, a radio personality on *Of Your Money*; and Ralph Hahmann, author of *Pension Paradigm*.

Clearly, mentors helped me to define goals, create timelines, and stay accountable. I want you to find financial success, and that starts with tapping into the wisdom and experiences of others. If you would like to speak with me about mentoring, contact me at www.BenardHD.com.

WHAT IS A BLUEPRINT?

A blueprint is a planning tool or document created to guide you in the process of building or creating your financial success. It can include your priorities, projects, budgets, and future planning. It can be revised, but serves as a guide to help you understand where you are in your financial journey. You can also make adjustments or fine-tune it on a daily, weekly, monthly, quarterly, or yearly basis. This is because various factors in your life can change. My divorce was one such event, but I am sure that you can think of many other examples.

You could win the lottery and be a millionaire, or you could lose everything that you own to a natural disaster. Heaven forbid, you could get into a car accident and sustain severe injuries or, worse, lose a family member to death.

The point is that, whether you recognize it or not, we all have a financial blueprint, from the homeless man on the corner to the wealthiest CEO. It might be a conscious or unconscious thing, but it does exist. Others have it written down. What I am about to teach you can be written out by a 7th grader. Many of us don't have money problems per se but have accumulated a lot of debt and expenses.

I believe that if we learned this strategy in 7th grade, it could create a shift in how we handle our finances, allowing us to avoid the large amount of debt that most individuals carry today. What a difference we could create for the next generation by teaching them about saving and investment wealth accumulation, the difference between good and bad debt, and more. The point is that what you are doing now is based on what you were taught in the past. Yet, that is not going to help you to create the future that you want. The past doesn't equal the future.

HOW DO YOU CREATE A FINANCIAL BLUEPRINT?

Throughout this chapter, I am going to give you the tools to create your financial blueprint. I just want you to remember that you are trying to keep things simple, so don't be afraid of having to make adjustments along the way. As Raymond Aaron says, just keep failing forward. The important thing is to just do it!

You are starting on a journey, and you need to draw the map that will help you to reach your final destination. The phrase to do expresses motion or moving in a specific direction towards a person, place, or thing. The point is that you have to take action. Right now, you have to get out a pen and a piece of paper. I want you to get everything out of your head. Start with creating four quadrants, as seen in the diagram.

Next, I need you to collect information together, so you know how much debt you have and how much income you have, such as income statements, investment income, etc. When you do your first financial blueprint, I want you to go low on income and high on expenses. As you do the math, you will be able to see whether you are cash flowing positively or negatively.

Most broke people go high on income and low on expenses, then they wonder why they are part of the 80% of Americans struggling financially. Now that you are reading this chapter and committed to changing your financial future, you are on the way to creating meaningful change in your life.

The definition of do is to perform an act or duty, to execute a piece of work, to accomplish something, or to complete or finish it. I want you to see this financial blueprint as a means to complete the action of understanding your finances, so that you can make informed decisions now to create a different future.

It is up to you to do the work. I am merely here to provide guidance and inspiration as you follow the directions to complete your financial blueprint.

INCOME

I

OWE

O

N
E
T
W
E
A
L
T
H

Gross=

Net=

Min=

Target=

Outrageous=

Accomodation=

Transportation=

Entertainment
& Communications=

Meal=

Spendings=

Deductible=

N/D Now Deductible=

$

$

ASSETS

A

LIABILITIES

L

N
E
T
W
O
R
T
H

Value=

Minimum=

Target=

Outrageous=

Financial=

Legal=

Deductible=

N/D Non/Deductible=

$

$

I OWE AL

My uncle Al gave me a simple way to do a financial blueprint formula. He explained that what goes in must go out. It is like breathing. The body must take in oxygen, in order to expel carbon dioxide. The concept is so automatic for us that, without even thinking, all of us take regular and consistent breaths throughout the day. Here is what is interesting, however. When we take the time to do conscious breathing, where we mindfully concentrate on how we breathe, suddenly the whole tone of our breathing becomes different.

You get more out of it, and your mindset shifts. You sharpen your focus and it proves to be beneficial to bringing peace to your mind and body. There are many different ways of creating this focus, a sharpness of the mind. I can think of several, including yoga, stretching, meditation, and more. The point is that you are creating an internal focus that can help you to achieve anything that you set your mind to.

The formula is I.O.A.L., Income (I), Out of Wealth (O), Assets (A), and Liabilities (L). Each of these areas is part of what you need in order to create wealth and grow your net worth. I am going to cover each of these areas and help you to understand this formula and how you can use it to benefit your financial plans.

INCOME (I)

What is income? Strictly speaking, it is the money that you bring in, either through your job or investments. Consider this the way that you breathe in, drawing in the financial capital you need to pay for your lifestyle, including your basic needs and your wants. Another way to look at it is the money that an individual receives from a company in exchange for goods and services. You are exchanging your hours and skills for dollars. The reality is that your income is often capped by the number of hours you work in a day, the number of miles you can drive, or the number of customers you can serve.

Investing, on the other hand, brings in money but the exchange is not the same. The rich use money to invest and make more money, often while they are involved in other activities. Instead of exchanging their time and skills, they are providing capital, and that means their income truly can't be capped.

Most of us think of our income in terms of what we make in an hour, multiply it by the number of hours worked, and then do the math to come up with our annual income. Yet, the reality is that you don't make that much. The amount that you did all the math to come up with is just a gross number and doesn't reflect what you actually get to spend.

What you need to focus on instead is your net income. This income is essentially what you bring home after you pay taxes, health insurance, and any other deductions. You might find that, in the end, your annual salary based on your hourly wages is significantly higher than what you actually bring home on your paycheck. Why is this important to understand?

Simply put, many individuals make spending decisions based on what they make in gross income and then wonder why they are struggling to pay the bills or meet their financial goals. They are focused on the wrong number, and its negative impacts their ability to grow their net wealth. Let's start by determining what your net monthly income is. I want you to write down every source of income that you receive on a monthly basis before taxes and deductions. Once you have that number, you can then subtract your taxes and deductions to come up with your net monthly income.

Now that you know what that amount is, it is time to look at where that income goes. Remember, many individuals plan their expenses based on their gross income, which means that they are going to find themselves in the hole every month. How often do you find yourself struggling from paycheck to paycheck, barely getting by, let alone putting yourself in a position to save and invest?

I want you to understand that just by acknowledging that there is a difference between your gross and net income, you are already ahead of so many individuals who are exchanging hours and skills for dollars. This is because you see the potential to rid yourself of the cap that comes with exchanging hours for dollars, and see the possibilities to increase your income with no limits.

When you choose to invest, it needs to be from the head and not the heart. Too often, people fall for a great story, but a poor business plan. Don't be one of them!

Pick your investments with an eye to the bottom line. What is the business plan, and what types of capital do they need to achieve it? Do their financial statements reflect a good use of capital, or do they struggle to make ends meet?

Consider using the Rule of 72. Einstein, who believed that one of the wonders of the world was compounding interest, came up with the rule. He explained that if you divide 1 into 72, then you get 72. So, if an investment pays 1% of interest, then it will take you 72 years to double your money. Now if that same investment paid you 72% interest, then it would only take you one year to double your money.

Recognize that there are wealth killers. These are taxes and inflation. Working with professionals, you can find ways to legitimately reduce your tax bill. Inflation, however, is not something that you can easily control. Therefore, in the Rule of 72, it is important to use a 3% percentage for inflation. Essentially, now you divide 3 into 72 and you come up with 24. That means in 24 years, the price of everything will have doubled. Therefore, when you are determining whether an investment is a good idea, you have to think about whether your return will be greater than the inflation during the same period. If not, then it is not going to help increase your wealth but may actually decrease it.

It is a question of finding the right type of investments that can work for you, based on your investment knowledge and risk tolerance.

Additionally, certain investments can create a greater tax liability based on the percentage of income earned. Therefore, you need to work with a tax professional to determine the best ways to legally minimize your tax bill through deductions. You may also choose to sell an investment to keep your income percentage lower and thus reduce your tax liabilities.

Many individuals argue about the amount of taxes they pay, or see them as excessive. I am not saying that those things might not be true, but at this point, governments depend on the tax revenue paid by their citizens. Here is a point that I thought was interesting from the New Testament of the Bible. Jesus was approached by the Pharisees and asked whether he should pay a temple tax. Now the Jews had no love for Roman taxes, and Jesus knew that their motive was to try to trip him up.

Instead, Jesus had one of his disciples pull out a coin and he asked whose face was on the coin. When the Pharisees responded that it was Caesar, Jesus responded, "Render therefore unto Caesar the things which are Caesar's, and unto God the things that are God's." The point? That taxes and the expenses associated with them are what we render to the government for the services it provides. At the same time, we can render receipts or other documentation to reduce what we owe, just as I am doing to have a $20,000 tax bill adjusted.

Therefore, whether you like it or not, these taxes are going to reduce your gross monthly income for years to come. However, there are ways to reclaim some of that money through your tax-deductible expenses. Working with a tax professional, you can find the best way to do so, recognizing that there are legal ways to effectively reduce your tax bill.

Another point to remember is that not all income is created equally. What do I mean by that? You have interest income, wage income, and rental income, for example. Each of those can result in a different tax rate, with different deductions that are applicable, as well as different rules for what must be reported. Recognize that you need to understand where your money is coming from to achieve the wealth goals that you want in your life.

Our next section is going to focus on Out of Wealth Expenses (OWE), which is where the income meets the expenses.

OUT OF WEALTH EXPENSES (OWE)

Your income is your wealth, and it provides you a means to pay for the things you need and want. These expenses typically reduce your wealth over the course of the month. When you think of this aspect of the blueprint, think of it as breathing out, expelling your financial capital in a variety of ways.

Take a moment and write down all of your monthly expenses. The list is going to include your mortgage or rent, utilities, car payment, insurance, internet, cell phone, and whatever else drains your income throughout the month. There are also those incidentals that you don't think about, because they have become automatic. Your stop at the coffee shop in the morning for that amazing latte? Out of wealth expense. Your regular lunch out with your workmates? Out of wealth expense. These little expenses can add up significantly over the course of a month. You might want to consider making note of every dollar you spend over the course of the week. You may be surprised at how much money simply disappears without you being consciously aware of it.

Remember **ATEMS**:
A – Accommodations
T – Transportation
E – Entertainment
M – Meals
S – Spending

Each of these has an impact on your budget. For instance, accommodations often take the largest chunk of your budget, with transportation next, then entertainment, communications, data, meals, and other spending. This type of spending could even include buying chocolate from a child for a fundraiser at school. Other expenses can include everything from lottery tickets to coffee and medical bills.

Now, there are other expenses that many of us deal with. Student loans, credit card debt, and perhaps even medical expenses. All of it adds up and can significantly reduce your income. There are ways to reduce those expenses, including refinancing loans for a lower interest rate or reducing your credit card spending. You also need to find ways to pay down debt faster, because this will save you money in the long run. What do I mean by that?

Most debts involve paying some form of interest on the debt. It is how the lenders make money from the individuals that they lend to. Now some interest rates are smaller than others, and obviously, the better your credit score the lower the interest rate is likely to be. Why? Because the higher credit scores are seen as lower risk to the lender, hence they receive the benefits in terms of lower interest payments.

However, when your credit score is lower, your interest is typically higher, and it costs you more to borrow money. The best way to save money on interest is to pay more than the minimum and apply as much as possible to the principal of the loan. Doing so will reduce the amount of interest paid over time. I have seen several examples of individuals who end up paying thousands of dollars in interest on their credit cards, simply because they refuse to make more than the minimum payments. Do not fall into this trap.

The best way to save money on interest is to negotiate a better rate, and always pay more than the minimum. When you are offered great credit offers, be sure to read the fine print. You may find that if you cannot pay the balance in full by the end of the term, you may be facing higher interest fees.

Once you pay down debt, it is important to keep it down. There are two types of debt: the type that is for non-assets and the debt for assets. The reason this difference is key is because, when you create debt to buy assets, you are building your net worth. When you grow non-asset debt, you are actually reducing your net worth and lowering your wealth.

If you have written all those expenses down, including food, gas, and what you spend on clothes, then you know what your out of wealth expenses are. Is that out of wealth number lower or higher than your net income? If it is higher, then you are in good shape and can start looking for ways to increase that income even further through investing.

However, if your net income is below your out of wealth expenses, then you are going to have to make some adjustments before you can start actively building wealth. The first step was already done when you listed all your expenses. Look over that list and don't make anything safe. Everything has the potential to be cut. For instance, those coffee shop visits? Perhaps they need to be on the chopping block to give you back more of your net income.

Anything that is an expense should be on this list, but keep in mind that choosing your expenses can mean you save money, or you might find that you are spending more than you need to in terms of taxes.

Look at your credit card debt. Are you getting your credit cards paid down, only to spend on them again, perhaps even drawing them over the limit regularly? All of these areas are places that you can start to reduce your out of wealth expenses. The point of this exercise is not to deprive you of the things that make life enjoyable, but to look for ways to make your net income and your out of wealth expenses balance. Eventually, the goal is to make sure that your out of wealth expenses are significantly lower than your net income.

One of the ways to do so is by tracking your expenses. If an expense is tax deductible, keep the receipt and then use that deduction when you file your taxes. To do this effectively, keep all your receipts and then separate them with your accountant into two piles, tax deductible and non-deductible. You might be surprised at how many deductions you have that you may have never claimed before.

Understand that money for business-related expenses is likely to be tax deductible, but personal items are not. Pay cash for personal items and then borrow for business expenses, thus allowing for the interest paid on business loans to be a tax deduction.

Think D=Deductible and ND=Not Deductible. Clearly, you can see the benefits of being a part-time business owner, even while you are an employee. Still, to be sure that you are getting all the tax benefits from your deductions and to determine which ones you qualify for, please consult with a tax professional.

Why do you think the rich become rich and stay that way? Because they tailor their lifestyle to a portion of their net income and then stick to it. They look for means to bring down their tax bill and do the recordkeeping necessary to achieve that. Additionally, they look for ways to increase that income, which leads me to Assets (A).

ASSETS (A)

To put it bluntly, assets are what you could sell to pay your debts. It could be your home, your car, or other valuables, such as jewelry. All of these items are assets. Your ability to purchase new assets can be based on your net income, but purchasing assets allows you to grow your net worth.

Investments can be a way to create assets. For instance, you might have $100,000 to invest. Now you could buy a rental property free and clear for that amount, or you could take that same amount and use it for down payments on four other properties. The result is that you have significantly increased your net worth by the value of those assets, but you have also increased your monthly net income due to the rental income.

Assets can be collateral for loans, or a way to get a lower interest rate. Home Equity Lines of Credit (HELOC) are a great way to maximize the asset you have in your home. You can pay the interest only or pay the whole amount off at any time. It allows you flexibility to invest in additional assets over time.

Assets are a critical part of building your wealth. I like to think of them as an acronym for the types of investments out there.

- **A** – Accumulating
- **S** – Several
- **S** - Stocks
- **E** – Estates
- **T** – Trusts
- **S** – Securities

Note that the point of accumulating these things is to create wealth, by the income they produce and the value they have against the debt that you might carry to purchase them. Choosing your investments wisely can help you to increase your assets and positively impact your net worth. Every investment has a level of risk, but the point is to balance your level of risk with the return from that investment.

In real estate, for example, you are focusing on being cash flowing on a property. That means the property covers its own expenses and still provides a positive income to you. I want you to remember that investments will have losses from time to time, but the point is that you don't want to have to continue to put income into an investment, because if it is not increasing in value, you are losing money.

I want you to get off your ass and do something to achieve something.

Are you willing to step outside of your comfort zone and try different investments? It might include spending assets to build your own business. The value of the business can grow, thus giving you an asset for your hard work.

I pointed this out because your ability to grow your income and purchase assets will be limited by your net income. When you work a traditional wage job, it caps your net income by the hours you work and the size of your paycheck. I am here to tell you that business ownership can mean taking your net income and growing it with no cap.

Now you might not be comfortable running a business, or you might be unsure of how certain things work when it comes to running a business. However, that is why you need to be willing to work with professionals. They can supply the knowledge and experience you lack. Plus, you don't want to be doing every job involved in running a business. You do not have enough time or energy to achieve all of that. The term is delegating, and it is key to any successful business.

Remember, you are doing something to achieve the wealth you want. Start looking at business opportunities with a critical eye. What is the investment needed, and the potential rate of return? How long before the business would be cash flowing? You might find, for example, that a franchise offers you the ability to purchase a business with all the systems in place, which may reduce your initial investment. However, franchises can also limit your ability to make changes as you see fit.

Therefore, it is important to weigh your options before choosing a business to invest in or purchase outright. Plus, when you purchase a business, you take on liabilities as well. However, liabilities are littered throughout the different types of assets available.

Let's move on to Liabilities (L) and how they can impact your wealth.

LIABILITIES (L)

Part of the point of liabilities is understanding that they are the items that reduce your net worth and negatively impact your wealth. Granted, they might be necessary expenses, but the point is that they are reducing the amount of net income you have to build your wealth.

You can think of them as sunk costs, ones that you are not likely to recoup as part of your investments and wealth building strategy. It could be insurance, setting up a trust or will, and consulting with professionals to determine the best tax strategy for your circumstances. The point is that these expenses are not going to be recovered, but the amount of these expenses also needs to be monitored. You might find yourself spending more than you should on sunk costs, and that can negatively impact your wealth.

However, the real liability is when you lie about your abilities, and you limit what you are capable of. So, you take advice from broke friends and family members, instead of consulting with those individuals who are professionals and experienced in generating wealth. Here is where I want to encourage you to look for mentors or coaches, and follow them.

They have experience and knowledge that you might not, but they also can help you to capitalize on the knowledge and experience that you already have. These mentors have walked the path that you are starting down, and can be critical to helping you achieve your goals and objectives. These are the individuals that can give you encouragement, and can also hold you accountable for achieving what is possible in your life.

CREATING TARGETS TO ACHIEVE YOUR VISION

When it comes to creating more income, you want to have several different targets. I think of them as the minimum, the medium, and the maximum. The minimum is essentially what you are making as a net income right now, factoring in wage increases or perhaps additional investment income. Now you might set your minimum as slightly higher, so you have a goal to shoot for in terms of increasing your net income from month to month.

The medium is a larger goal, outside of your comfort zone, that makes you have to hustle a bit to achieve it. You might take on an extra project for additional income beyond your job, or you might find yourself investing more. The point of medium is to make you stretch yourself further than you have before. To achieve your goals in terms of growing your wealth, you need to be willing to step outside of your comfort zone. Medium goals are meant to be a driver for that. At the same time, when you achieve a medium goal, you feel the rush that comes from accomplishing something and it pumps you up. Suddenly, you can see that more is possible. That is where the maximum comes in.

Now I have heard this goal referred to as outrageous, but the point is that this goal means you are really going to have to stretch yourself and take a gigantic leap outside of your comfort zone. It might even mean completely changing your lifestyle to break the barriers keeping you from reaching that maximum goal. From month to month, you are going to be able to reach plenty of minimum goals and even a few of the mediums, but you might think that the maximum goals are just too far out of reach.

I am here to tell you that is not the case. In fact, every time you reach a medium goal, you put that maximum goal closer and make it easier to reach. Even if you don't achieve it right away, you don't feel like a failure, because you achieved one of your other goals. The point is to put achievement on a sliding scale, making it easier to keep yourself pumped up to achieve the financial goals and dreams that you have always envisioned.

Part of this process involves changing how you think about building wealth. You want to use your income to generate future income. Your wealth is going to be tied to the investment choices you make and how you use those investments to essentially fund the purchase of future investments. If your investments have investments of their own and you are living off of that income, you are generating a consistent income stream that will positively impact your net wealth for years to come.

As an investor, you also have the opportunity to have your money start making money for you by using a professional. It is important to remember that there are individuals out there who spend their days working hard at finding the right investments to fit a variety of circumstances or investing goals. They are going to listen to your vision and help you make smart investment choices to achieve it.

Interview people and find the ones who are successful. For instance, if you decide to use a financial planner, ask how much they made last year. If it was less than you, then that is not the person you want working with you, because he is broke! You want to work with successful people to achieve your own success.

One of the key points I want you to understand from this chapter is that, as an employee, everyone is benefiting financially but you! Self-employed individuals pay the same tax rate as employed individuals, but they get to take deductions not available to employees, plus they have a more flexible schedule. Business owners get even more deductions and tax incentives. Optimize your income by owning a business. If you are thinking that owning a business is time-consuming and you don't have the time, consider hiring a general manager to run the business for you. For more information about the benefits of business ownership to your financial success, visit my website, www.transformationalblueprints.com.

Then you receive the benefits of owning the business, while being able to collect the income and still pursue what you enjoy in life.

Your circumstances can also change throughout your life, meaning that your financial vision is altered as well. Working with professionals can help you to keep your investments in line with your vision, even as it changes throughout your lifetime.

CREATING YOUR FINANCIAL BLUEPRINT

Finally, I want to discuss how this all can impact the life that you live. Many of us have dreams and goals, but the financial realities are limiting us from achieving them. I want you to be able to live the life you have always dreamed of, and fulfill your purpose. To do so, you need financial resources. When you choose to work with a financial professional, you get access to someone who can help you to achieve the financial resources necessary to achieve your dreams.

You have the ability to create an amazing life, but you have to believe that you are worth it. Once you make that conscious decision, then the next step is to define what amazing is to you. Everyone's idea of an amazing life is different, depending on their own personal experiences, beliefs, and values.

I want you to take a minute and define an amazing life for yourself. I can give you one example of how I value myself, and what I believe is a critical part of my amazing life. I always travel first class. Now, it is more expensive than a seat in economy or business class, but I value myself and see it as a priority not to spend hours cramped as I fly. Granted, this might not be one of your priorities, but that is what makes this part so interesting. All of us are unique, and so each of our lives can be amazing based on those unique aspects.

Get excited about the possibilities. Define your amazing life and then act to create it. If you wait for someone else to give it to you, you will be waiting a long time. My mother is still incredibly active, living life to the fullest. It is an example that inspires me to get the most out of every day of my life.

I also want to stress the importance of finding support to create real change in your financial life. After all, it isn't going to be easy to change how you view money, how you interact with it, and how you invest it. In fact, you might be so focused on just paying this month's bills that you can't even imagine life more than 30 days from now. That is the mentality that you need to break. It takes conscious effort to create that mental change, to shift your mindset.

After all, it took years to create the habits and mindset that are now your automatic default. When you change the default, it takes time to make it permanent. To be successful at it, you must get started. Financial shifts require effort as well, but they are so worth it. Do not be quick to assume that you can't do it! Instead, focus on the blueprint and your action steps in each area. Perhaps you just focus on one area at first, then shift to another. Over time, you will see the change, and its impact on your life.

Throughout this chapter, I have shared key strategies and important information that can help you through the process of creating wealth and growing your net worth. It comes down to a simple formula, one that requires you to think in terms of algebraic equations. (And you said that you would never use that again!)

Income – Out of Wealth Expenses = Your Net Wealth

Assets – Liabilities = Your Net Worth

These two points are essentially your financial blueprint. No matter what you do financially, it fits into one of these four categories. The point is to make smart choices that positively impact these areas and thus increase your financial wellbeing. Go to BernardI.O.A.L..com to find more information on how this financial blueprint can help you to achieve success.

What are some ways that you can make real change in these areas? Let's look at all of them one at a time.

- **Income** – Look for ways to increase your income through investments or business ownership. These options allow you to use your money to make more money, instead of just putting more hours in at a job. Remember, you can only work so many hours a week, which naturally limits how much income potential is available at a traditional job.

- **Out of Wealth Expense** – Choose your priorities and then work to manage your out of wealth expenses. Always remember to live within your net income, not your gross income!

- **Assets** – Building a portfolio of assets is key to growing your net worth. Choose your assets, not only for their current value, but for how those assets can grow over time. Work with a professional financial manager to help you invest effectively to increase your net worth and build income streams that allow you to live the life you want.

- **Liabilities** – Not all liabilities are the same. Some are the result of doing business, including insurance and legal or tax guidance. Limit liabilities that drain your resources unnecessarily.

Each of these areas is part of making your finances what you need them to be in order to achieve an amazing life. I have focused on your mindset, on your choices, and on ways you can create real change. However, they all require you to get up and move. You need to act, to embrace your abilities, and focus on what you are capable of.

Too many of us sell ourselves short and end our lives wondering what we missed out on, because we did not embrace our abilities and talents. Don't make that mistake!

Granted, you might not be interested in an investment because it doesn't mix with your values or it is not going to get you where you want to go in the timeframe you have already defined. The point is to explore the options and find the ones that work for you.

I met a wealthy friend who told me about a great book, Rich Dad Poor Dad by Robert Kiyosaki. That book opened my eyes to so many concepts that before had appeared complicated. It was as I read his book and took inspiration from it that I had a better understanding of income and how to generate it, as well as the tax implications of that. Today, I help people determine the best investments based on their goals, helping them to understand how each income presents different tax rates and more.

Now is the time to act. Don't put it off until tomorrow or some future date that will never come. Instead, open your mind to the possibilities.

Years ago, a friend interviewed for a position as an office boy. It was going well, until she asked for his email address and he explained that he didn't have one. She politely said they couldn't use him, and that was the end of the interview. Instead of allowing a fear of rejection and the accompanying dejection take hold, he decided to get active.

He had $10, so he went to a wholesale fruit distributor and bought a bag full of produce. He then sold it door to door. That day, he doubled his money and a new venture was born. It took time, but he went from walking to riding a bicycle to owning a truck and then a fleet of trucks. His hard work created a viable business. Now, he could have let that interview bring him down but, instead, he used it as inspiration to move forward. I want to provide that same inspiration to you. I want to help you act to create your vision. Don't let the rejection get you and keep you from fulfilling your dreams and goals!

Let's get started working together as a TEAM (Together Everyone Achieves More). Please contact me at my website, www.transformationalblueprints. com, to create real change in your financial life, and discovering the resources to fund the amazing life that you deserve! In this chapter, I have shared how to map out your financial plan, creating a You Are Here point in your life. Now I need you to transform this moment, getting rid of what no longer serves you by transforming your thoughts and feelings, essentially exhaling your negative thoughts and emotions.

Part of that process involves taking action. What do you want to be known for at the end of your life? Name three things. Now is the time to create and build, so use those three things as a platform to get started. Let them help you to craft your mission statement and the theme song of your life. You are in control of your mind's eye, your dreams, and your creativity. These are the tools that will allow you to reach your destination and leave a legacy behind for generations.

Practice conscious bio-breathing. Take a moment to think about what you love, and then hold that breath and truly experience your thoughts. Recognize that in that very moment, there are thousands of cells are being born in your body! All those cells with be filled with the energy and information captured in your DNA. Now exhale on the negativity in your life, including jealousy, visualizing the cells dying and leaving your body within the time it takes to exhale. It is all mind over matter. If you don't mind, then it don't matter!

Life is a journey of experiences, but you are the one who takes those experiences and crafts them into a truly amazing life, one that will be a legacy for others to follow for generations!

Please go to www.transformationalblueprints.com to download the I.O.A.L. chart and to get more information and details about Bernard H. Dalziel.

www.ingramcontent.com/pod-product-compliance
Lightning Source LLC
Chambersburg PA
CBHW060541210326
41519CB00014B/3300